WHY YESTERDAY TELLS OF TOMORROW

Helmut Gaus

Why Yesterday Tells of Tomorrow

How the long waves of the economy help us determine tomorrow's trends

Garant

Helmut Gaus
Why Yesterday Tells of Tomorrow
How the long waves of the economy help us
to determine tomorrow's trends
Leuven - Apeldoorn
Garant
2001

170 p. - 24 cm
D/2001/5779/99
ISBN 90-441-1205-8

Cover design: Koloriet

Garant
Tiensesteenweg 91, 3010 Louvain (Belgium)
Koninginnelaan 96, 7315 EB Apeldoorn (The Netherlands)
uitgeverij@garant.be

Contents

• Foreword

The less one knows about history, the more puzzling the future seems. If we look at changes in values and mentality over a longer period, we end up with a demonstrable theory that is meaningful not only for an understanding of the present but also enables us to make explicit statements about the future and past behaviour of the masses.

The hypothesis we formulate for the first time in this book substantiates the prognostic and historical value of this theory, namely that social development is being determined by the cyclical course of a common feeling of anxiety. We can observe that, deep down in the subconscious of the masses, uncertainty and anxiety increases over a period of twenty-five years and subsequently decreases over a period of twenty-five years. There is reason to believe that we are dealing here with an autonomous process that is influenced neither by the economy nor by any other development but fundamentally affects human behaviour.

Many will immediately ask which inferences we can draw from this for the present era, in which we are at the beginning of a long decreasing wave of anxiety. What direction will the change of values take? What changes of mentality can we expect? The reader who is interested in these questions could go straight to the last chapter. But readers who attach some importance to scrutinising the scientific credibility of this theory and checking the tenability of the resulting statements, will need to start from the beginning.

Mindful of the publisher's wishes, we have written a short, accessible version to allow those who are not practised readers of scientific works to enjoy it.

In the first chapter we clear the way. In other words, we ask the question of what might trouble us as soon as we are confronted with a new theory, especially when it is based on results drawn from different fields of science.

The second chapter recapitulates the theory of the "long waves", which the Russian statistician Nicolai Kondratiev unlocked to a broad public. Kondratiev had calculated that during one and a half century, wholesale prices in the industrialised Western countries had fluctuated in cycles of about half a century, twenty-five years up and twenty-five years down. Without knowing it, he had discovered the long wave of anxiety. After Kondratiev, many have tried to find in the economy itself the causes of this remarkable cyclical movement of prices and, by extension, economic cycles. In vain, we would say, and clearly self-evident, since the turning points are to begin with a phenomenon of mass psychology and not of the economy. This of course implies that the economic cycles are being determined by the long wave of anxiety.

When we know how important anxiety is in social development, we want to know precisely what anxiety and uncertainty are. This we can learn from the psychologists although each of us knows these feelings from personal experience. Chapter 3 tries to answer the question. We will not enter at length into pathological forms of anxiety but examine increase and decrease of ever-present anxiety, not of the individuals but of the masses. It also puts into the psychological sphere certain situations that we will develop later, more concretely, in the social sphere. It does not always make a world of difference, but still.

Chapter 4 attempts to formulate a theory that provides a connection between concrete behaviour and the deeper-lying psychological needs. The relevance of this may not be obvious to everyone. However, underlying uncertainty and anxiety, or its opposites, creates masses of needs, which manifest themselves in concrete behaviour that cannot always be straightforwardly identified as anxiety-driven behaviour. With this theory, our view of society becomes bifocal. Through the upper half of the bifocals, we see concrete behaviour, through the lower half the underlying needs and emotions. We need bifocal lenses to get a clear understanding of the long wave of anxiety.

In chapter 5, we search for reliable indicators of social anxiety. An earlier study (1992) has shown that the colour preferences and certain characteristics of women's fashion as we can see them in women's and fashion magazine, form a very reliable indicator. What is more, they can be seen as the long wave itself. In this chapter we specify to what extent other behaviour — such as, for example, investments in the last half-century — reflect the long wave of anxiety. Following on from that, we present the remarkable correlation between particular fashion trends and Kondratiev's figures from the end of the 18th until the 20th century. It was to be expected but is still astounding. With this material, our initial hypothesis becomes even more workable.

In chapter 6, we will be looking at our society today and tomorrow through the upper half of our bifocals. What changes of value can we expect during the long phase of ever-decreasing uncertainty and anxiety that has commenced in the last decade? The low point of uncertainty and anxiety — the term non-existence would be too strong — or, in the words of Kondratiev, the peak of economic boom, should be situated in the next decade.

To conclude, we would like to express our warmest thanks to Jacqueline Van Hoe, who has over the years acquired extensive statistical knowledge of the fashion world. Her knowledge is infinitely richer and more thoughtful than chapter 5 could show. Considering their importance, a separate publication of her findings is unquestionably essential. Her captivating interest in the subject has more than once been an important support. Last but not least, our thanks goes to Elke Matthyssen who has kindly shouldered the responsibility for the statistical part and with whom we had exciting discussions about the efficacy and shortcomings of particular statistical procedures in the case of long time sequences concerning people's behaviour.

We also wish to extend our thanks to the Censydiam Institute and in particular to its chairman Jan Callebaut for the trust he has at all times put in our research and the support he has given.

Helmut Gaus

1. Tuning our violins

I hope that the theory drawn up in this book is false. I fear that it is correct.

As soon as we are confronted with a theory, we react to it on the basis of our individual background, knowledge, opinions, preconceptions we already have in our heads, and so on. All this will determine our overall judgment of the theory. When people from different disciplines — i.e., with very different academic backgrounds — are confronted with the same theory, their understanding and judgment will largely be determined by these backgrounds.

That is why it seemed useful to bring to mind some fundamental facts that will play an important role in the theory we will develop here, facts with which everyone is familiar in some way or another, and tune our violins.

Our first important string concerns the subconscious. Our theory is rooted in the fact that a major part of our behaviour is not determined by reason but by subconscious processes. The Swiss psychologist Carl Gustav Jung expressed it concisely when he said that consciousness was an island in the sea of the subconscious. The German philosopher Friedrich Nietzsche meant the same when he said that all thought is second-hand. In other words, before anything comes to the surface of our consciousness, it was already there. Many motives behind our behaviour are not the result of conscious thinking. For a psychologist this is, of course, as evident as can be. There are quite a few people however who will raise their eyebrows when they hear this. Is reason no longer the only true instrument of explanation? If we are forced to explain our behaviour to another person, we will hardly ever admit that we do not really know why we behave in a particular way. We will try to find a rationalisation and, in addition to that, we will — unwittingly — seek an extra rationalisation that we — subconsciously — suppose the other person will understand and accept. Whether these rationalisations are true or not is another question.

If it comes to "lying" to ourselves and to others when explaining our behaviour, we are — for very functional reasons — great masters. This may be evident to everyone but, though we are confronted with it every day, it is not wholly pointless to repeat it.

When studying human behaviour, one is constantly confronted with behaviour for which the person concerned will give an explanation that will not sound very convincing to others. "Why do you eat chocolate? — Why do you go on holiday? — Why do you hate foreigners? — Why have you put shutters on your windows? — Why do you find that politician X does a good job and politician Y does not? — Why do you find principles important sometimes and not at other? — Why are you interested in the fate of kings and princesses?" We will readily find an answer to these questions, an answer we are rather pleased with, an answer that appears to be acceptable to us. But is it true? After all, who is interested in an answer that may be less obvious if we have one ready that seems perfectly true to us?

That is why we pay particular attention in this study to what people do and only sporadically to what they think and what they say. Behavioural information is our keyword. However, this sets the problem of how to interpret this behaviour, of establishing what it means. Furthermore: What is the accuracy of our interpretation? Which theories shall we use? All this does not make it any easier, as we shall concretely see.

In addition to this, we are not dealing with the subconscious behaviour of individuals but of the masses, or more correctly, of large sections of society. We are interested in individuals inasmuch their behaviour is representative of the behaviour of thousands of others. If in a span of a few years, groups appear in the political landscape that begin to worry about the environment, they display a behaviour that makes their views clear: periodicals will appear, associations will be formed, Green Parties will get thousands of votes, and so on. We call this mass behaviour because it concerns large parts of the masses. This is a convention. Accordingly, when we talk of behaviour of large sections of those masses, we talk in fact of averages.

Thus far our first string: we are dealing with the subconscious behaviour of the masses and primarily interpret it on the basis of behaviour and not on the basis of explanations given by the people concerned.

The second string relates to the distinction between human behaviour and the circumstances in which people live. This distinction is to some extent arbitrary but, then again, it is vital to our theory.

This is what we are talking about: on the one hand, there is the evolution of the circumstances in which people lived and live. The circumstances change over the years according to their own time and rhythm, such as population growth during the last 2,000 years, for example, and discoveries, inventions, and so on. The external context in which people lived 2,000 years ago is barely similar to the circumstances in which they live now. Which external circumstances do the inhabitants of a present-day village still have in common with the inhabitants of a Celtic village at the time of Julius Caesar?

If we assume that human behaviour is reactive, i.e. a reaction to the external circumstances in which people live, we must also assume that the constant changes of circumstances will result in a constant change of behaviour and that the behaviour of contemporary people is in no way comparable with whatever behaviour in the past. In this reasoning, all behaviour is non-recurring and so it does not allow scientific study in the strict sense of the word science, according to which uniqueness is a contradiction in terms. Proceeding from this vision one could indeed argue that Brutus murdered Julius Caesar on one occasion only. Yet, if we want to make a scientific study of regicide, we can start with Caesar and end, for example, with John F. Kennedy. So we can compare hundreds of regicides from the past. A subtler example will make it clearer still. Someone can strike up an exceptionally precious friendship and be convinced that such a thing is possible only in our era — until he reads Cicero's *About Friendship*, which was written 2,000 years ago. A lover of nature could read Virgil's *Bucolica*. For want of a more adequate definition, we could say that there is something such as "typical" human behaviour, which is constantly present, no matter in which era, but not always in the same form.

The suggestion that there are constants in human behaviour that can be traced back to Roman or even prehistoric times conflicts with two tenacious preconceptions of our era: the preconception of linear progress, which, since the end of the 18th century has replaced the idea of a more cyclical evolution, and the preconception that we have become the "smartest" in history today (simply because we are still alive and the others are dead). These two preconceptions prevent us from learning anything from human behaviour in the past and call behavioural historical science a utopia. For the most part, however, these preconceptions are implicitly rather than explicitly present; they are hardly ever conscious. The past is an immensely rich laboratory of human behaviour. The contemporary, living human being cannot imagine behaviour that would not have hundreds of parallels in history. The central theme of this book is anxiety-driven behaviour in the present and in the past, and it could well happen that more than a few people will be prepared to accept — in spite of all preconceptions — that it is almost certainly a subject for all eras.

The third string concerns repeats, or recurrences, or models, or systems of human behaviour, or whatever one wants to call them. On the one hand, it is a subject everyone is familiar with in daily life, but on the other hand it is also a delicate subject, depending on the discipline in human sciences. In the science of history, it has no more than a few supporters whereas it is widely accepted in psychology and in sociology. In historical economics, it is the very basis.

In fact, what does it mean? Simply that people's behaviour consists of many repetitions, recurrent behavioural patterns, which can even be represented by models. Social scientists generally content themselves with finding these recurrences — which is no easy task in itself, considering the continually changing parameters. Yet, recurrences in human behaviour are so much more important in view of the study of prognoses and, in history, retrognoses, too — by which we mean "prognoses in the past." For example, if we find certain behaviour in a certain context, similar behaviour must have occurred in similar contexts in a distant past.

In everyday life, we incessantly observe our fellow men. Slowly but surely we see certain patterns of behaviour recur: certain ways of thinking, of acting, of reacting — things which taken together we often call "someone's character," and which, after all, is a construction. With this knowledge we can make the prognosis that if such a person, with these personality traits, finds himself in a certain situation, he will very probably behave in the way we already know. As a science, psychology is based on this principle. Deviant behaviour is observed and then we study how someone who shows such deviant behaviour behaves. After studying a number of cases, we assume that someone with such an abnormality will display this behaviour — which is a prognosis.

The remarkable thing about this is that, at the level of the individual or of small groups, one is ready to accept, and also use, these recurrences, whereas one is much more reserved when large groups or masses are concerned. Some persist in quoting from Gustave Le Bon's *La psychologie des foules*, an obsolete work from 1895. We leave aside prognoses concerning the evolution of whole cultures, because prognoses necessarily concern human behaviour *and* the external circumstances in which this behaviour is displayed; they cannot be separated. Immediately above we argued that one could not make prognoses about the two together, according to the same scheme. Whether the West will decline, as Oswald Spengler says, or civilisations will clash, as Francis Fukuyama predicts, are questions that also imply prognoses about the evolution of external circumstances. Well, I do not have the faintest idea of how to make a prognosis about the discovery of nuclear fusion with tap water as a new source of energy, for example, though it would have immense consequences for the evolution of the whole world.

The only ones who, since the beginning of the 20th century, have always kept a watchful eye on the behaviour of groups over a longer period with a view to finding recurrences, have been economists, with Nicolai Kondratiev in front. Kondratiev is so important for the rest of our story that we will devote a whole chapter to him. Yet, his findings have not only been adopted in economic sciences but also outside. Just look at the divisions historians have been making when writing about recent history: time and again, we find the same divisions Kondratiev discovered in the evolution of certain economic processes.

Despite the fact that it is an academic subject, making prognoses about the future course of specific social-scientific aspects of behaviour is a risky undertaking. Serious social scientists do not want to gamble their name and reputation by making prognoses that could turn out to be incorrect. People would see it as a proof of very poor scholarship.

Yet, methodological and practical research in this direction has been carried out to satisfy the needs and demands of the market. Indeed, business undertakings want information on future production and distribution of goods and services. Some marketing firms have managed to explore and deepen their research into personality traits and the ensuing behavioural characteristics and fine-tune it to very specific segments of society. They have found out that we lack the underlying fundamental theories, which allow us to prognosticate long-term macro-social changes, whereas since Freud theories about the behaviour of individuals abound.

The fourth and last string we should tune, if only briefly, to facilitate a good understanding of this theory, concerns a rather philosophical category, namely determinism. The moment one develops a theory about a workable system concerning the behaviour of groups and masses over a long period, people almost automatically ask: So are we subject to determination? From the way in which the question is put, it appears that people are not happy about this. They have reason to be despondent, as we are effectively subject to determination, at any rate that is what I think. We are subject to determination in the sense that we act according to certain mechanisms which we do not know and which we therefore do not try to influence consciously.

Simple prognoses — for which we will have to run ahead of our story — such as the prognoses that tell us that in the coming twenty years fear of death and concern for our health will sharply decrease, that the number of children in families will increase, that women's liberation will expand enormously, that the colour black will completely disappear from our clothing, and so on, and this on the basis of a fundamental mechanism in the development of our society, all this sounds pretty much like an unpleasant deterministic mechanism. Many would prefer it not to be true. When one reads this book assuming such an attitude, it is obvious that criticism and final judgment are... determined in advance.

This is a fascinating problem in itself, which, unfortunately, we cannot study in greater depth as it is too far removed from our subject. In fact, individual psychology does nothing but establish behavioural mechanisms. As we already said, establishing recurrences in behaviour is elementary scientific research. In fact, establishing that someone with specific personality traits will behave in this or that way under certain circumstances is also determinism. We all have a certain amount of freedom of action, within certain limits, but we cannot go beyond these limits, or only a little. These limits basically determine everyone. Nobody will be irritated when we say that a child who grows up in a family that speaks a particular language is "determined" to learn that language. If we say that in a phase of long-term economic boom — in which we are now — the number of children per family will increase, some will raise their eyebrows.

It is obvious that the attitude towards determinism and the acceptance of any behavioural mechanism do not come out of a clear blue sky like the Coca-Cola bottle in the famous South-African film *The Gods Must Be Crazy*. Since the Industrial Revolution and the French Revolution, our culture firmly has believed in absolute freedom of speech and action, which is contrary to any idea of determinism: *Liberté, égalité, fraternité, ou la mort*. This unbridled ideology of freedom was an absolute condition for future economic evolution, and so it became a new determinism, an ideological determinism in fact, for the development of the 19th and 20th centuries.

In conclusion, we should say that if behavioural mechanisms are a fact, we should not reject them, since there are only two options that remain. Behavioural mechanisms exist, but we do not know them, and we refuse to get to know them because they reduce our freedom to an illusion. In the latter case, our freedom depends on our ignorance: the more ignorant we are, the more we are free. On the other hand, we could accept them — or at least not exclude them — and, because of that knowledge and after we have surveyed all our determinants, try to find out how much freedom, if at all, remains. The more we know, the more precise is our insight into true freedom. Ignorance or knowledge at the service of freedom: a difficult choice?

2 The enigma of the long waves in the economy

When we look for regular patterns in the behaviour of — preferably large groups of — people and over longer periods, we find ourselves in the field of economics. Economics is one of the few social sciences that has so many precise calculated facts available with respect to social evolution over extended periods. Economic historians have calculated the cost of bread and rent over centuries, back to antiquity.

Early on they arrived at the conclusion that the economic process — which is, of course, the result of human action — shows regular patterns which at first sight are not easy to explain. They are all the more remarkable because the patterns appear to be cyclical when obviously nobody could have planned a recurrent cyclical pattern. These patterns seemed to have occurred spontaneously, similarly to people who have mastered a language and later become conscious of the fact that underlying this spontaneous usage there is a strict grammar whose presence they never suspected.

The exceptional importance of cycles in this specific human behaviour is obvious. Cycles are recurrent phenomena and have a high probability of reoccurrence in the future. So they are not only important in explaining the past but can also form a basis for the study of the future. It all depends on our insight into the nature of these recurrent processes. Is this cyclical character only a matter of economic processes or is it a matter of broader social facts?

1. Early interest in cycles

Before Karl Marx had published his economic works, the interest in the study of economic cycles was not at all evident. With the Industrial Revolution arose a form of linear vision of the future, which gave the impression that the past could best be forgotten. The Industrial Revolution was the beginning of a new development that was putting society in situations unlike ever before, faster and more comprehensively. Cyclical thinking however implies studying that "history repeats itself" and was at odds with the new era.

As early as 1857, William Langdon, founder of the Manchester Statistical Society, noted that commercial fluctuations followed a ten-year cycle. John Mills pursued the idea and found, in 1867, that the periodic commercial crises were being caused by the destruction — in people's minds — of a bundle of opinions and beliefs. (Glassner, p. 437) W.S. Jevons endorsed this view and wondered which elements could cause such changes of mood with such regularity; he came out with the theory of sunspots.[1]

In his analysis, John Stuart Mill concluded that for one reason or another optimism is reversed and prices begin to fall. So here the recurring element was a psychological factor. (Glasner, p. 434) In 1857, Samuel Jones Loyd, ennobled as Lord Overstone and, at his demise, described by *The New York Times* as the greatest contemporary authority on trade and finance, took the view that all economic fluctuations formed an actual cycle and that it was an inescapable characteristic of the market economy. Periods of crisis were followed by periods of prosperity or, as he expressed it, "by states of confidence." The cycle was simply the consequence of psychology and not of any other structural fact of the capitalist system. S.J. Loyd (Glasner, p. 409) arrived at this conclusion in the middle of the prevailing view that crises occurred rather irregularly and sporadically and thus were not a recurrent phenomenon. It is remarkable that these authors give psychological factors such an important part in the explanations of prosperity and crises.

2. The four cycles

Today, four cycles have been identified: a three-yearly, a ten-yearly, a 25-yearly and a fifty-yearly cycle, i.e., the Kitchin cycle, the Juglar business cycle, the Kuznets cycle, and the long wave of Kondratiev.

In 1923, the British statistician Joseph Kitchin discovered the existence of cycles of economic activity of more or less forty months, cycles that had not

1 John Mills, *Credit Cycles* (1867). Quoted in: S.J. Peart, *Mills, John, 1821-1896*, in: D. Glasner, op.cit., p. 437. See also S. Peart, 1991.

been identified before, and longer cycles of seven to ten years that were already known. He based this on numerical data of the period 1890-1923 in Great Britain and the United States. This cycle is also called inventory investment or the minor cycle.

Clément Juglar had already calculated the cycle of 9 or 10 years at the end of the 19th century but did not uphold the regularity of the cycles and ultimately extended the span of his cycles from two to five years, which make the use of the term "cycle" rather dubious. However, the remarkable thing is that Juglar based his cycles on a history of crises as early as 1696 and on the cyclical patterns of marriage and birth rates in France. We will follow him there in chapter 5. After Juglar, several authors found trade cycles with intervals of about ten years, or credit cycles of the same length, which in this case justified the use of the term "cycle."

In 1939, Joseph Schumpeter integrated both cycles with his noted three-cycles diagram. The three-cycles diagram assumes that fluctuations in economic activity are determined by the short Kitchin cycle of 40 months, the half-long Juglar cycle of nine to 10 years, and the long Kondratiev cycle of 48 to 60 years. The three cycles are superimposed, so to speak, and can reinforce each other if they take the same course or weaken each other if they take the opposite course. In the meantime, the Kuznets cycle, also called the building cycle, which was drawn up by the American economist Simon S. Kuznets and bears on American economy, seems to have passed out of use.

We should add that all these authors generally designate economic processes as the causes of these cycles and so attribute an endogenous development to the cyclical events. In other words, economic factors cause the rise and fall of the economic cycles.

We will ignore the shorter cycles because, as far as we can see now, they do not have a clear impact on social processes other than the economic and can therefore be seen as truly endogenous cycles.

3. The discovery of the long wave in economic activity

The long wave of Kondratiev's cycle however is a cycle that runs parallel with a great number of distinct social behaviour and social changes. The continued existence of this wave should allow us to expect the same or similar changes in the future. It is the only one deserving our attention.

There are questions about the exact dating of the peaks and lows according to which economic time-series one uses. There are questions about its cyclical character; in other words, one sees the rising and falling of economic activity but one wonders whether its course is in effect regular. Finally, there are questions about its cause. Countless theories have been proposed which all in their own way tried to explain what causes these long waves of economic activity. If one wanted to contribute to the study of the causes, one had in the first place to accept the long waves.

In view of the importance of this wave, it seems to be indicated to have a closer look at its development and it seems useful to point to an essential methodological aspect. We must make a clear distinction between describing these cycles and trying to guess at their causes. The fact that one cannot explain them in a simplistic way is not to say that they could not exist.

On the basis of studies of long time-series of prices, interest rates and trade movements, a number of economists, including V. Pareto, have put forward the fact that half-century wave-like movements existed in the development of the capitalistic West. Acting on this, Pareto predicted, in 1917, that after the war a prolonged period of recession would follow, a prediction that was obviously forgotten during that period.[2]

Today, it is generally accepted that it was the Dutch Marxist economist and later professor J. Van Gelderen who, in 1913, in the socialist magazine *De Nieuwe Tijd*, under the pseudonym of J. Fedder, tried to give the first description and explanation of the phenomenon. Van Gelderen had assembled facts from the period of 1850-1911 and thought he could affirm that the period 1850-1873 was characterized by an acceleration, the period 1873-1895 by a slow-down, and the period after 1895 by a new acceleration.[3] However, due to the unknown pseudonym and the fact that it was published in Dutch, this contribution went completely unnoticed by foreign colleagues who were dealing with the same question.

2 J. Kuczynski (1987), referring to V. Pareto, "Forme di fenomeni economici e previsioni" in: Rivista di scienza bancaria (1917)

3 J. Van Gelderen under the pseud. J. Fedder (1913), cf. J.J. van Duijn (1979, pp. 29-30)

There is also the contribution, in 1914, by M.I. Tugan Baranovsky, which was published in German in 1901 and in French in 1913, and the Russian Marxist A. Helphand, published under the name Parvus. Apart from them, there is M. Lenoir, about the formation and evolution of prices and the 1913 publication by A. Aftalion on the generalized and periodical crises of overproduction.[4] It is not surprising that the first such studies came from the Marxist quarter. In his overall economic work and especially in *Das Kapital*, Karl Marx had been referring to fluctuations that ranged over long periods. Apart from this, without specifically referring to long waves, he had pointed to the cyclical character of the economy. Marx himself, however, had his doubts about the possibility of the capitalist system recovering.

4. The discovery of the long wave by N.D. Kondratiev and his contemporaries

The recession that set in after WWI aroused wide interest in the study of long waves. It was a 1925 publication by the Russian statistician Nicolai Kondratiev that gave the phenomenon of long waves its name.[5]

At the age of 25, Nicolai Kondratiev, born in 1892, became undersecretary of state for food in Kerensky's provisional government. From 1920 until 1928, he directed the Moscow Institute of Applied Economics, which he had founded. During that period, he worked chiefly on agricultural prices, which enabled him, in 1923 and 1924, to set up the first Five-Year Plan for agriculture. At the same time he worked on long waves. His interest had probably been roused by the work of Tugan Baranovsky, whom he held in high esteem and who had already worked in that direction.[6]

4 M. Lenoir (1913); A. Aftalion (1913 and 1927, 2 vols.)

5 Vincent Barnett (1998) has written a sound study of N. Kondratiev. The fact that he has read numerous publications in Russian adds greatly to its importance.

6 N. Jasny (1972)

Kondratiev himself was cautious about the interpretation of his long waves. He based his first conclusions chiefly on the long time-series of prices. In this respect he declared, in 1922: "We regard the long waves in the capitalist economy only as a probability." In a more comprehensive analysis he published in 1925 and which was based on long time-series of prices as well as on production figures, he called long waves "very probable." In this analysis, Kondratiev did not yet concern himself with a possible explanation of the wave-like movement. He did that in a lecture at the Moscow Institute of Applied Economics, which was published in 1928. In this, he limited himself to a reinvestment cycle of long-life capital goods. In the same year, he lost his position as head if his Institute and shortly afterwards the official Soviet encyclopaedia threw out his long wave as "erroneous and reactionary." In 1930 he was arrested and, after a show trial, deported to Siberia and executed there in 1938.

The periodisation Kondratiev had developed in 1925 distinguished the following phases:

First long wave:
- Ascending phase from 1780 until around 1810/17 (1789-1814)
- Descending phase from 1810/17 until 1844/51 (1814-1849)

Second long wave:
- Ascending phase from 1844/51 until 1870/75 (1849-1873)
- Descending phase from 1870/75 until 1844/51 (1873-1896)

Third long wave:
- Ascending phase from 1890/96 until 1914/20 (1896-1920)

The years between brackets are turning points in price movements. It needs to be underlined that, as said before, an important distinction has to be made between establishing the existence of the waves and their explanation. Many authors unintentionally confuse or mix up both elements and begin to doubt their validity to the extent that their explanation becomes more problematic — which we will see below. Kondratiev himself was basically concerned with determining these long waves though he put them in a wider context and distinguished the following characteristics:

- during ascending periods the years of prosperity are more numerous whereas in a descending phase years of depression predominate.

- the problems in the agricultural sector are particularly acute in descending phases.

Graph 2.1: Kondratiev's wholesale prices (completed) USA, 1749-1939

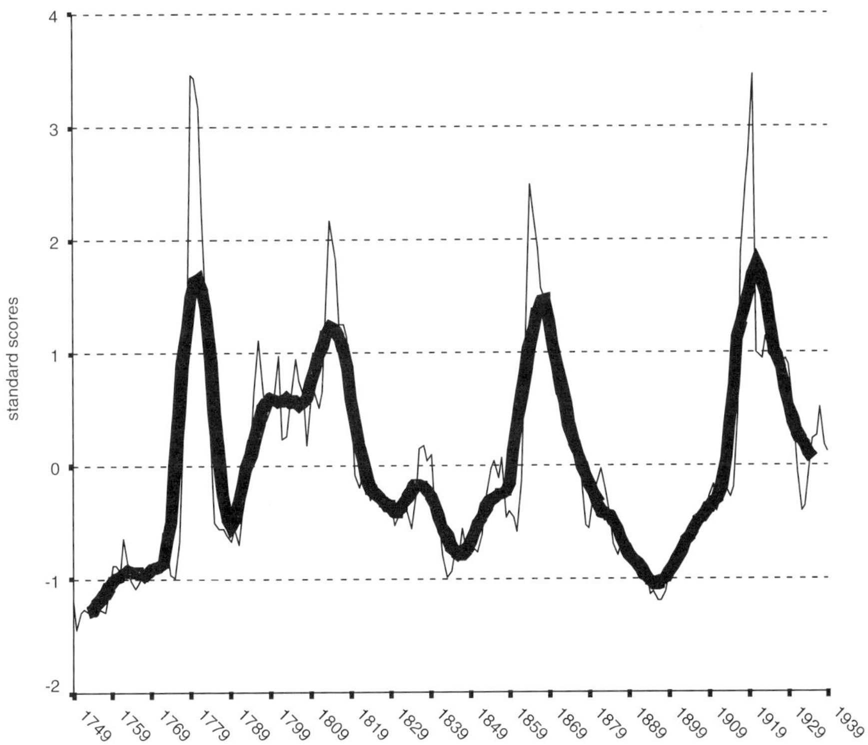

Per annum and 9-year moving averages
Source: Kondratiev and Mitchell (1993)

- during the descending phases many things are being invented that will for the most part be applied during the following ascending years.

- at the beginning of an ascending phase the production of gold increases and the world market for goods has usually improved owing to the assimilation of new and especially colonial goods.

- wars and revolutions mostly occur during ascending periods.

It is important to note that Kondratiev argues that these changes are the consequence of economic processes, of endogenous factors, and not of

Graph 2.2: Kondratiev's wholesale prices (completed) England, 1750-1939

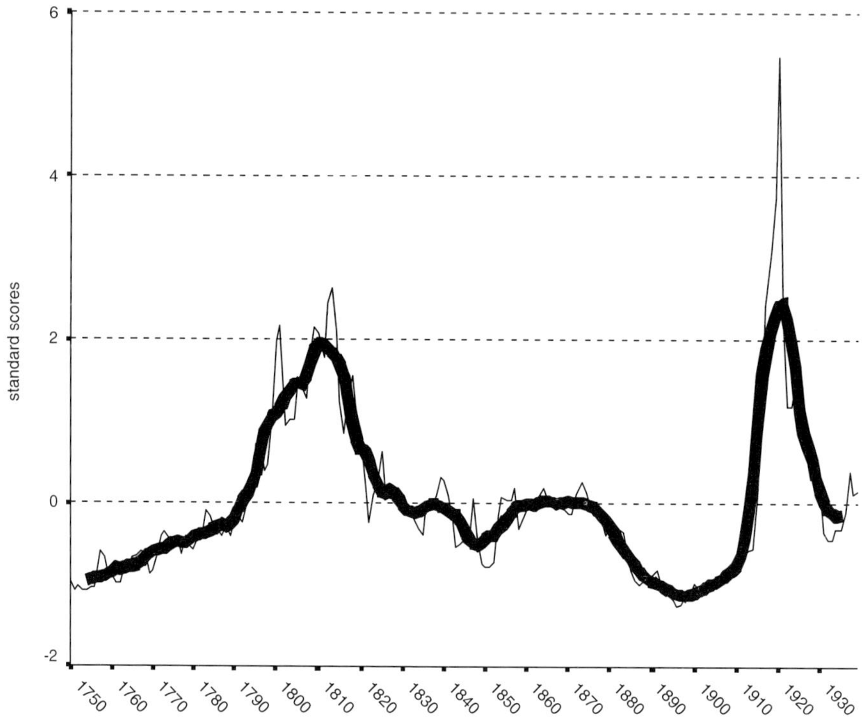

Per annum and 9-year moving averages
Source: Kondratiev and Mitchell (1996)

factors that lie outside the economic process. Wars too are the consequence of factors that are inherent in the economy and, principally, by the increased tension caused by the economic fight for markets and raw materials. The odd thing about it is that he juxtaposes wars and revolutions.

Despite the tide of criticism against long waves, we have to acknowledge that Kondratiev initiated the debate that provoked an avalanche of publications during the depression of the Thirties — publications that did not survive WWII though. The ascending wave, which swelled during the Thirties and would last until 1971, has shut out as it were the reminiscence of descending phases. Then, however, when a new recession loomed, there was a renewed interest in the study of the long waves. We can agree with C. Freeman when he writes: "If one of the tests of a theory is predictive power,

Graph 2.3: Wholesale prices (completed) Belgium, 1832-1939

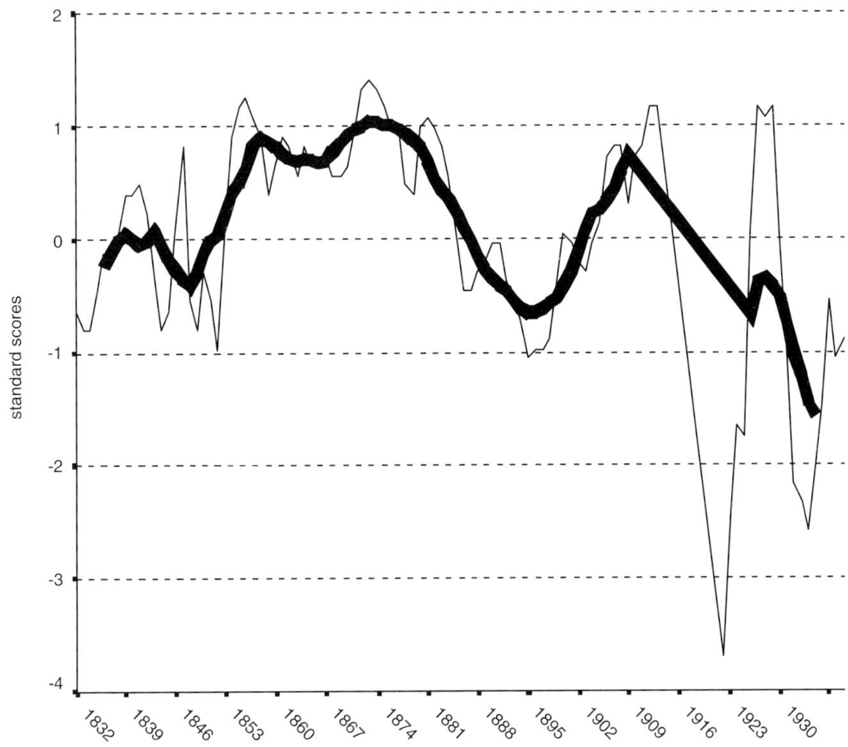

Per annum and 9-year moving averages
Source: Mitchell (1993)

it must be said that Kondratiev's analysis, advanced in the 1920s, gave a rather reliable forecast of the main trends in world economy over the next sixty years."[7]

We need not go deeply into the study of long waves before noticing that the study of the long waves itself is subject... to long waves. During ascending economic trends, they are hardly ever mentioned. Mentioning long waves

7 C. Freeman, *Long Swings in Economic Growth*, p. 241

during periods of expansion would seem like doom mongering. During descending periods however the mechanism of long waves is most likely to be discussed to get an insight into the duration and hence the possible end of the long descending wave one is going through.

When we review the history of the 19th century superficially and compare it with the periods Kondratiev has described, the waves seem odd and even enigmatic. Indeed, their true meaning is defined by the very viewpoint from which one looks at them. If one looks at them from the viewpoint of the art historian, the descending periods appear to be romantic and emotional whereas the ascending periods are more realistic. If one views them from the standpoint of the polemologist, all great wars appear to have taken place during an ascending period or at it's peak: the Napoleonic wars at the peak of the first long wave, Bismarck and the French-German war at the peak of the second long wave, the Great War during the ascending phase of the third long wave. The interest in nature is a product of Romanticism, which corresponds with the descending period of 1811 to 1847; the second burst of interest in nature is evidently typical of art nouveau, which manifests itself at the low point of the third long wave, in 1896. The same low point gave us a first upsurge of anti-Semitism in France — the Dreyfus affair — followed, in Germany, by a second surge in the Thirties, i.e; the third low point of the long wave, which of course passed by Kondratiev in his Siberian exile. The national figures of marriage, vocations to the clerical order, and so on, show, as far as we can determine for the 19th century, the same rhythm as the long wave.

The better we know history, the more it becomes clear that the long waves — which are in themselves a reflection of economic fluctuations, of the prices in particular — are associated with social change, which on the face of it has little to do with the economy. One can of course invoke a rather rudimentary Marxism, which has otherwise proved its validity, that is to say that its economic data (the infrastructure) can influence very many cultural and psychological facts (the superstructure). In other words, that economic prosperity, or economic depression, can perhaps have an effect on xenophobia, on demographic data such as marriages, on war, and so on. However, the fact is that, firstly, these economic changes must precede all others moving to the same rhythm as the long wave and, secondly, the question remains whether it is the long wave itself that causes the economic changes. In this matter, the chronology is more important than had first been suspected.

Can economic cycles and all other changes that move to the same rhythm be caused by a third factor that lies outside these facts? That is a fundamental question. If we found out, for example, that non-economic social trends such as demographic figures, art-historical data, and so on, run parallel with or even precede the long waves of economic fluctuation, we do have a problem with the Marxist model: How can the infrastructure influence the superstructure if it changes earlier than the infrastructure? Then there is the fundamental question: what is the exterior cause that gives the economic cycle as well as the non-economic trends their — roughly speaking — fifty-yearly rhythm? Is it the change of generations, which usually span 25 years, as a result of which a full Kondratiev cycle would encompass two generations? What attention did authors give to this in their assertions?

5. The usual explanations of the long wave

Explanations of the long wave circulate which are, on the face of it, quite logical and easy to accept. If we start from a low point in the economic cycle, we can assume that at that moment entrepreneurs begin to see markets. They begin to invest with a view to increase their production, a phenomenon that also begins to appear in many other sectors. This gradual process is then accompanied by increasing demand and increasing consumption, if only as a consequence of increasing employment. Not only in private industry but in public services too, we see an increasing tendency to invest. We see a positive climate and the whole process of production, investment, and consumption begins slowly but surely to run. Until, with the lapse of time, the market becomes saturated: profits become smaller, competition becomes more oppressive, investment decreases because consumption decreases or no longer keeps in step with production. The phase of overproduction has come. This process too takes time before reaching a dead-end and the economy slumps into depression, with high unemployment, low consumption, low investment, a high savings quota, and a continuous fall in prices. The deadlock will eventually be broken by some captains of industry beginning to reverse their attitudes and, with an eye towards a possible increase in consumption, begin to invest again, picking up where they left off; we have come full circle.

This does not explain the moment of reversal, the swing. Why do some entrepreneurs suddenly begin to look to the future in a positive way while depression and depression indicators remain the same? Indeed, it amounts to a manifest negation of the negative economic facts that prevail at that moment. Why, during a decreasing phase of the long wave, is there an impulse to consume more and why do entrepreneurs, almost at the same time, feel the need to invest? And why do we see the reverse during the phase of economic boom, since there are no clearly visible signs of a slump. Why the sudden atmosphere of prudence, of restraint, of decreasing consumption, of saving, of fear for the future, and so on?

A historical fact is explained only when we have explained why it occurred and why it occurred at exactly that moment.

Therefore, it is useful to see which factors have been taken into account in the past to explain the long waves. It will enable us to look more closely at two aspects. Is it a perpetual motion theory, a theory that tries to convince us that in the economic process each phase is the cause of the next and therefore would explain the cause of the descending or ascending trend of the long wave as an endogenous economic process? This would allow us to assume that the cycle must inevitably continue but for catastrophic outside interference. How this explains the purely economic functioning of the process is only partly important as far as this question is concerned. The reason why a recession, once it has started, becomes increasingly bad and eventually turns into a depression, or why an incipient upturn continues to go upward, can probably be explained in a large measure by the endogenous causal chain of economic factors. In this, the explanation of the moment of reversal, of the change in trend, at the peak as well as at the low point, is at the forefront.

The question is whether there are theories that also invoke exogenous factors to explain the tide of the wave at its highest or lowest point. We will look more particularly at the extent to which the pioneers of the theory have invoked mental and psychological factors. By doing this, economists tread on dangerous ground, since the vast majority of them are non-professionals in the field of mass psychology.

To begin with we must also express our astonishment at a sort of lack of methodological "hygiene." Unfortunately it appears that studies of the long waves — i.e. the Kondratiev waves — always involve business cycles and, conversely, that studies of business cycles also involve long waves. All this while there is no dispute about the fact that as far as the latter — formerly called Juglars — are concerned we are dealing with 10-year cycles and the long waves span 50 years. With the best of intentions, the causes that would be workable for the explanation of a 10-year cycle cannot be used to explain a 50-year cycle. When studying the long waves we should rigorously separate the singularities of each cycle.

6. Dating: the end of the 19th century and the beginning of the 20th

Table 2.1: Dating of the long waves

	-	+	-	+	-	+	-	
Kondratiev (1926/35)	1789	1811	1847	1871	1896	1921		
Mandel (1975)		1827	1848	1876	1894	1914	1939	UK
			1849	1974	1894	1914	1939	USA
			1850	1875	1898	1914	1939	Germany
		1820	1840	1870	1891	1913	1938	world trade
Imbert (1959)	1787	1817	1851	1872	1896	1926	1935	France
	1791	1814	1849	1865	1896	1920	1932	USA
	1792	1808	1849	1873	1895	1925	1933	Germany
	1786/9	1810	1849	1873	1896	1920	1933	UK
			1852	1873	1895	1929	1934	Belgium
Simiand (1932)		1815	1850	1875	1896	1928		France
Dupriez (1947)	1789	1811	1848	1872	1895	1920	1939	
De Wolf (1924)		1825	1849	1873	1896	1913		
Hansen (1941)	1787	1815	1843	1873	1897	1920		
Woytinski (1931)		1822	1842	1873	1894	1920		
Ciriacy-Wantrup (1936)	1792	1815	1842	1875	1895	1913		
Kuznets (1940)	1787	1814	1843	1870	1898	1925		
Burns and Mitchell (1946)	1789	1814	1843	1864	1896	1920	1932	USA
	1789	1813	1849	1873	1896	1920	1933	GB
		1820	1851	1872	1896	1926	1935	France
	1793	1808	1849	1873	1895	1923	1933	Germany
Rostow (1978)	1790	1815	1848	1873	1896	1920	1935	
Van Duijn (1983)			1845	1872	1892	1929	1948	
Dupriez (1951)	1791	1818	1844	1873	1898	1913		

Source: J. Goldstein, 1988

In *Long Cycles: Prosperity and War in the Modern Age* (1988), Joshua Goldstein gives us a neatly arranged schematic representation of how different authors have dated the long waves. We have used it as a basis for the outline below.

First, we should note that the use of precise dates is not entirely correct. When we find ourselves in an ascending or a descending phase of a 50-year wave, choosing one single year from these phases — even if we base this on economic data — is rather arbitrary. However, since we are faced with calculated time sequences, such a choice is possible. On the other hand, not all parameters used to calculate the ascending or descending waves indicate the same peak or low years. In addition to that, there is the fact that in the main industrialised countries peaks and lows will sometimes differ by some years. For this reason, it is advisable to regard the dates as relatively approximate.

7. Problems with dating the long wave in the 20th century

The question now is: what is the course of the long wave in the 20th century? If we may situate the peaks in 1921 and 1971, the long wave is actually even more cyclical than we might have expected. Indeed, between the first and the second peaks, 1811 and 1871, between which lie 60 years, the subsequent peaks follow each other with an awful regularity at intervals of 50 years: 1871, 1921 and 1971. If the cyclical course continues in the same manner — and with every wave the chance of it increases — we will reach the next peak in 2021. However, as we said, exact dates have only a relatively limited value. A descending or an ascending phase covers several years.

We may hesitate about the 1921 peak, which some situate before the Great War and others later. Explanation? The following low point is situated in or around 1933, which would imply a very short recession of no more than 12 years and a very long ascending period from 1933 until 1971, which after all, as already said, makes 50 years in all. The problem is to be found in the descending phase. Two authors, E. Mandel (1980) and J.J. Van Duijn (1983), situate the low point after 1945 and this makes a huge difference, as the prologue of the Second World War and the war itself fall ahead of the low point. On the other hand, with the low point in 1933-1935, the prologue and the war itself are situated in the ascending phase.

However, the peak of 1971, or 1973, is hardly ever disputed. Until now, there is little literature on the following low point and little will be published yet, on account of the psychological mechanism that almost totally obscures interest in the possible end to the booming economy. We will talk later about the problem of the 1970 peak and the low point around 1990; we have been able to calculate them on the basis of totally different data.

We are left with the low point during or after WWI. Most data prompt us to adopt the viewpoint of Nathan Mager: "The contemporary Kondratieff wave is generally regarded as having begun in 1949, when the U.S. economy returned to a normal postwar pace, although the trough of the third wave occurred in 1932." (1987, p. 140)

We will not enter at length into the many statistical discussions based on different figures. The work of Reijnders (1990) sounds very convincing. After all, we are dealing with waves of human behaviour over a period of almost a century and a half, which cannot be approached in an all too mathematical way.

We believe that there is a relatively large consensus on the dating of the long waves and only the two world wars lead to divergent opinions among some authors.

8. Some explanations of the long wave

Gold or money reserves

Nobody will deny that gold and money reserves are an important factor in the economic process. The discovery of important gold reserves in the world in the second half of the 19th century, at the beginning of the ascending long wave of 1847, and then again at the beginning of the ascending wave in 1896, has created the assumption that these discoveries have caused the ascending trend of the economy. The reduced monetary importance gold has these days eliminates this factor. The deflationary monetary policy that a number of countries adopted between the world wars to halt the crisis was prompted by the conviction that monetary policy can have a significant impact on the economic process. Today, the monetary policy of a country remains an important driving force of the economic process, by setting the interest rates, for example. However, this contributes little to the explanation of the cyclical character of the long waves.

Wars

As we said before, invoking wars as a factor that would cause an ascending or a descending wave is hardly defensible. It is a factor that is strongly tied to the times of the researchers themselves.

Papers invoking wars as explanatory factors were almost all written between the two world wars. After the lasting peace in the West from 1945 until now, researchers are less inclined to invoke wars as causes of the long wave.

Innovations

When we talk of innovations, we are referring not only to the massive introduction of new distribution and production processes but also to improved goods and services. Theories saying that such innovations cause the long waves are in part based on the fact that important innovations have characterised every ascending long wave: steam power, railways, electricity, motor cars, computers. These innovations had already been partly developed during the preceding descending long wave but had not been exploited, given the context of the descending phase, when people had little inclination to invest, little confidence in the future, fear of high risks, et cetera. Schumpeter (1939) stated that innovations appear in clusters and that there are phases with many and phases with few innovations. Yet, in his fascinating description of the processes involved, Schumpeter does not give unambiguous reasons that should indicate why those clusters are suddenly and massively utilised and in other phases are left on the drawing board.

Capital stocks

Obviously, fluctuations in the production of capital goods are a field of research for the aetiology of long waves. There is the factor of the lifespan of capital goods and their periodic renewal. Even before the war, the regularity of the fluctuations in the production of capital goods had been recorded, yet without suspecting the causes. Forrester (1973), who has carried out interesting research in this field, sometimes needed an exogenous factor to adjust the erratic mechanism and in particular to bend the descending trend upwards again.

Price variations

As long ago as 1914, the Frenchman Jean Lescure, looking at the evolution of prices but also of interest rates, wages and ground rent, had discovered ascending and descending phases in the economy of about a quarter of a century each.[8] The first cause is the expansion that occurs in a sector of industry such as the railways or electricity and subsequently extends to other sectors. The descending phase sets in because of the decreasing gains in top sectors, which leads to a decline in investment, which in its turn further extends to other sectors. Like Van Gelderen, says Scandella, Lescure holds the view that the development of new industries is accompanied by the development of new countries, and further, that global growth is favoured by the growth of gold reserves. Lescure holds that the changes of profit margins are the key to the evolution of the long waves, the same conclusion that was reached later by Ernest Mandel. The question about all this is how it happens that the growth and decline of the profit margins prove to be so regular. In all fairness we should add that Lescure published his findings in 1912 and 1914, and that he had only the 19th century as a source, with only two peaks (1811 and 1871) and two lows (1847 and 1896) of the long wave to work on.

Saving behaviour, over and underconsumption

As early as 1917, V. Pareto had formulated the hypothesis that there was a connection between ascending and descending trends in the market and the greater or smaller amount of the savings balance. The high level of savings during a descending phase creates the conditions for an ascending phase, during which the amount of savings decreases, which creates a new phase of recession. However, why people, in each case, wait for a quarter of a

8 Jean Lescure is not mentioned in *The New Palgrave: A Dictionary of Economics* (1987) nor in David Glasner's *Business Cycles and Depressions* (1997). The index of Christopher Freeman's edition of thirty-three articles on the theory of long waves mentions his name only as a reference. We extracted the short survey of his views from a study by Luigi Scandella (1998), pp. 18-19.

century to spend their savings and consequently get an ascending period going or why they save more and cause a recession, remains an open question.[9]

Investments

As early as the end of the 19th century, capital investments have been invoked as an determinant factor to explain the existence and the fluctuation of long waves. In 1936 too, Keynes' General Theory attributed an important role to investments. The theory was couched in its definitive form by Jay Forrester of the Massachusetts Institute of Technology (1973), in the course of which two initial propositions of Kondratiev were adopted and developed. It is obvious that the nature and scope of investment have far-reaching consequences in stimulating or curbing the economic process. Yet, if we want to explain the cyclical character of the wave, investments have to increase or decrease periodically. This raises the question of the possibly cyclical character of the decisions by managers and governments to increase or decrease investments. It is clear that these decisions are closely linked to the positive or negative future expectations these people have, i.e. linked to sources of information but also to psychological factors. Daring, courage, but also the assessment of the risks, play an important role. Yet, daring and willingness to take risks are not constant factors; they fluctuate with time. This changes the phrasing of the question. We are not asking about the causes of increasing or decreasing investments but about the increasing and decreasing expectations, which clearly makes us leave the field of the economy, though not the field of the economists. As early as 1913, Irving Fischer sketched a theoretical approach to the formation of expectations in which price levels played an important role. Incidentally, it was this issue that inspired Keynes' famous concept of "animal spirits," being a collective term for the "historical, political, and psychological characteristics of an economy," whatever they may be. If one can ever demonstrate that investments indeed have a profound influence on ascending or descending trends in the economy, the ultimate question remains — sometimes as a lifelong preoccupation, as for the Polish economist Michal Kalecki.

9 It was Scandella (1998, p. 19) who pointed out this aspect of Pareto's theory.

9. Conclusion

If we review al these explanations, we come to the following conclusions. First, they reflect to a great degree the era in which they were formulated. Secondly, the endogenous explanations often form a circular process that suggests a perpetual movement, in contradiction to the dating of the long wave and the chronology. Thirdly, there is hardly ever space for the psychological side of human behaviour, which does not follow economic logic and cannot care less about the rational choice theory. There are quite a few authors though who are conscious of this shortcoming and do not attempt to disguise their inability to figure out this dimension of economic behaviour.

In this respect, the conclusion of the eminent scholar Jürgen Kuczynski is quite significant: "I have come to acknowledge the existence of long waves, without being able to find a satisfactory explanation for them in my own or other studies." (T. Vasko, 1987)

Jonathan Steinberg puts it differently: "As you would expect, economists and economic historians do not agree on the existence, the measurement and, above all, the causes of such long waves. Oddly enough, they do agree on the dates and for our purposes that is the most important part."[10]

This situation is perfectly understandable since it is not economic but psychological facts that are the real basis of long waves. This idea is not new either. The founder of the three-year cycle theory, Kitchin, has already propounded that the capitalist process only reflects the rhythmical movements of mass psychology. And if the cycles are less precise, he continues, this is due to the nature of human behaviour or to certain factors such as when food production deregulates the normal cycle. A brilliant idea but, to the extent that it is true, it proves that the explanation of the appearance of long waves can no longer be sought in economic data and will remain a permanent enigma for economists. In Kitchin's time, psychology was still in its infancy and the further development of that hypothesis remained impossible. On the basis of quite different and more subtle material from the second half of the 20th century, we are now

10 In: Financial Times, September 8, 1982, "Why the recession may last till 1996."

convinced that Kondratiev's waves are indeed a fact of mass psychology, and are more specifically waves of increasing or decreasing uncertainty and anxiety that indeed reverse every half century. Essentially, the evolutions that scientists who have been studying long waves have recorded need to be interpreted as the reflection of the long waves of anxiety on the level of the economy. It also entails that these waves, with all their ensuing behaviour, which can be seen as the exteriorisation of underlying uncertainties and existential anxiety as, for example, in certain fashion trends, can be reconstructed. Not surprisingly, they show the same patterns, in the 19th as well as in the 20th century. In consequence, the long waves cease to be an enigma. They would have remained so as long as one continued to search for an economic explanation.

In the next chapter, in order to develop this new hypothesis, we leave the field of economics, move over to psychology, and see what psychologists mean when they talk of anxiety and how it manifests itself. In the following chapter, we will try to link external behaviour with underlying subconscious needs, to which the economy of anxiety belongs. In chapter 5, we will come to the construction of the long wave of anxiety.

Graph 2.4: The long wave (idealized), 1789-2020

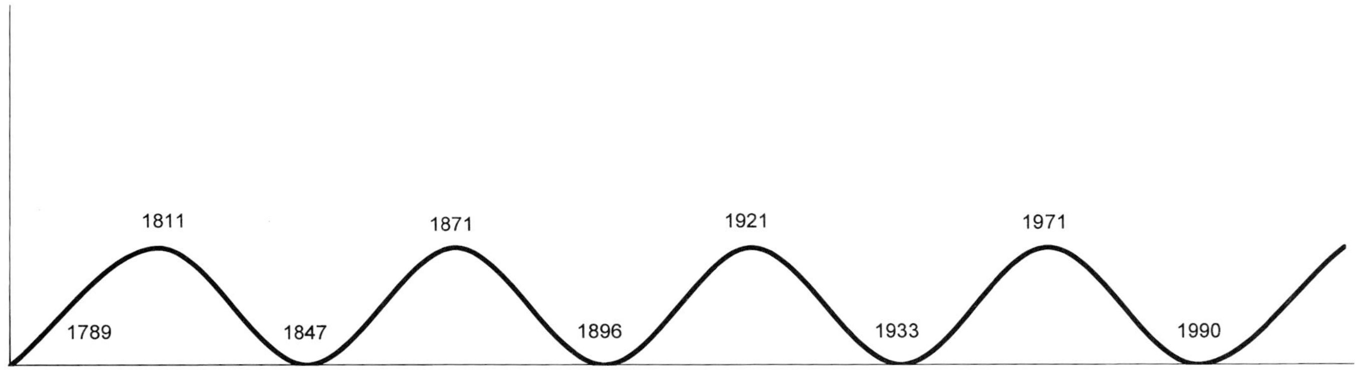

Source: see chapter 5

3. Anxiety and functional anxiety-driven behaviour: the construction of a model

Our theory says that Kondratiev's long waves are, basically, waves of anxiety, i.e., long-term fluctuations of the average level of anxiety in society. This theory calls for a review of what psychologists have to say about the matter. In the following pages we review the essentials and list what seems to be relevant for our purpose.

1. Why construct a model of anxiety-induced behaviour?

Everybody who is familiar with scholarly work knows that researchers almost invariably work with "models." There are very elementary models, such as notions and definitions, and very complex ones, which reflect the mechanisms of society, such as the "free market economy".

Considering the basic assumption that in prolonged periods of recession a good deal of group behaviour can be interpreted as the manifestations of a heightened level of anxiety, we need a model of anxiety behaviour. There are some problems though, as "anxiety" is a fairly complex issue. Specialists tell us an infinity of things about anxiety, much more than we need for a study of "normal" anxiety in masses, and, on the other hand, they do not tell us quite enough. It would be useful to point out clearly what we need and what we do not need.

In the first place, we need to describe the behaviour of someone who is anxious, i.e., his or her external behaviour that is clearly perceptible, including language, and, on the other hand, we need insight into psychological behaviour, i.e., how someone who is anxious feels. We do not need to know the physiological processes that occur in the brain and in the rest of our body when we feel anxious. Apart from that, every psychological experience and every form of anxious behaviour is an individual fact. However, we are chiefly concerned with the behaviour of groups and large sections of the population in the event of an increase in the level of anxiety in society. We want to know whether the understanding of individual anxious behaviour can also be used to understand anxious behaviour in large sections of the population. Expressions of anxiety that somehow cannot be socialized, i.e., translated socially, are quite irrelevant to our research and have no further value than helping us with the construction of the model.

On the other hand, there is the problem of the identification of group behaviour as an expression of anxiety. Let us give an example. Is a significant increase of interest in martial arts in many people the social translation of an increase of anxiety? It could be a social expression of anxious behaviour but on the other hand this kind of sport is part of the existing sports culture, which is also being practised in periods with low levels of anxiety; martial arts probably answer other needs too. Only a strong quantitatively increased interest, which runs parallel to times of increased levels of anxiety, can indicate that this sport would begin to be an anxious reaction.

It opens the question of bridging the study of the individual — with all his external and internal reactions — and the study of culture as a collective response to the needs of many individuals. Recognizing and interpreting cultural behaviour as just so many answers to individual needs and frames of mind poses a number of problems of its own with regard to reliability and verification.

Overall, more precise, more explicit insight into anxious behaviour is more rewarding methodologically. The assumption on which our theory is based is that in downward phases of long waves, large groups of people display behaviour that can be interpreted as anxious and, conversely, that this behaviour decreases when the wave rises. It is obvious that, when saying this, we are already basing our ideas, albeit implicitly, on a certain model of anxious behaviour, in which we see increased emotionality, forms of romanticism, and so on, as expressions of anxious behaviour. When implicitly setting up the model, the historical events of the last two centuries in general and the periods between World War I and World War II have been extremely helpful. Methodologically, however, it meant that we repeatedly "scanned" the spectrum of two centuries of history in order to see if we could detect long-term behaviour that could be interpreted as anxious behaviour along the lines of the implicitly constructed model.

A model of anxious behaviour based on psychology gave us a double advantage. First, the implicit model became explicit. Then, we could base ourselves on that model to explore history and validate the model. At the same time, we could set aside as being coincidental historical developments that showed the same rhythm as the long waves but had no direct or indirect relations with the model of anxious behaviour.

Finally, this methodological inversion — taking theory and not facts as a basis — required us to seek information in the present and the past to which no attention was generally paid as it was not relevant to the usual and current explanatory models whereas, in a psychological issue, it was of decisive importance.

2. Problems with defining anxiety

On a first acquaintance with "anxiety" in specialist literature, it is obvious that the construction of a model of anxious behaviour is not so simple.

Anxiety is an "invented" construction

Several problems are connected with the fact that the notion of anxiety is an abstraction. The term anxiety does not refer to anything concrete. Nobody has observed anxiety. We do experience specific feelings, with or without externally perceptible expression, with or without perceptible physical and neurological processes. All this together we call anxiety. Therefore, anxiety, like all other abstractions, is an "invented" construction.

Some authors see anxiety as a physiological and especially neurological fact. For others, anxiety is what one "feels" of it. Some others explore the "feeling of anxiety" in philosophy. Dependant on the basic principle, each definition contains important notions that in their turn have to be defined.

When one has to translate subjective experiences into definitions, one rapidly comes to the conclusion that one has ended up in a linguistic game. Replacing meanings with others does not make subjective experiences more objective.

The distinction between anxiety and fear gives us a good illustration. Some authors hold the view that one should make a clear distinction between anxiety and fear.[1] They say that the word fear should be used when one "fears something" definite, something that is known and demonstrable, whereas the word anxiety is used when the fear has no precise object and is therefore indefinable.

To escape — at least in part — from this linguistic game, and to be scientifically sound, one has to look at behaviour that is connected with a subjective experience we can describe with a notion or a concept. This means that we fall back on the behaviouristic view held by Karl Marx when he wrote that man is what he does.

Accordingly, we see that someone who is anxious, or who — by way of experiment — is put in a situation that makes him anxious, begins to sweat and that his pulse rate increases. Hence, one can say that a situation that one describes as fearful is accompanied by an increased pulse rate and transpiration. However, not everybody who transpires and has an increased pulse rate is anxious. For someone who studies the pulse rate it is totally irrelevant to know what fear "really" is. He sees an increased pulse rate and transpiration as parts of the definition of fear. (E. E. Levitt, 1968, p. 27.) As we can see, a behaviouristic foundation makes a rather weak basis for the construction of a model of anxious behaviour.

Etymology

It does not happen very often in psychology that the etymology of a word can be significant to its meaning. The etymology of the word anxiety, however, does tell us something. The Latin "anxietas" derives from "angere," to narrow, to compress, and to feel oppressed. In the word "angor" it also has the secondary meaning of depressiveness. The adjective "angustus" signifies narrow or tight. Yet, the origin of the word anxiety goes further back than the Latin, namely to the Indo-European stem "eng."

In contemporary Western languages, we find the same stem: "Angst" in German, "angoisse" and "anxiété" in French, "anxiety" in English, and so on. This dimension of the feeling of anxiety we get from the dictionaries is very meaningful and contains quite a few elements that we should hold fast

1 This distinction goes back to the work of S. Kierkegaard, *Der Begriff der Angst* (1844).

onto the model. The element of "being oppressed" especially is probably the primary cause of the increasing personal involvement during a period of increased level of anxiety.

Definition

At first sight, scientific definitions give us a good deal fewer elements than would be of use for a model of anxiety-driven behaviour.

As early as 1972, C. D. Spielberger advanced that anxiety forms a "pattern" of emotions, "a complex emotional reaction in which fear as well as other fundamental emotions are included." (1972, p. 10) In the same volume, Caroll Izard endorses this viewpoint: "a variable combination of interacting emotions." (Ibid. p. 52) The new element in this definition is that anxiety is not an independent emotion, easily separable from other emotions, but a combination in which anxiety — clearly represented as a separate emotion — is predominantly present. Izard has put forward a totally new criterion in opposition to this. He argues that he can distinguish certain emotions from others on the basis of neurophysiological processes. Izard appears to have identified these neurophysiological processes but, except for the assertion that anxiety is a combination of different emotions, it is irrelevant to our study.

Butollo (1984, p. 21) also shares Izard's suggestion that anxiety is a collective term for a great many emotions that have a certain number of aspects in common. Yet, Butollo adds: "We have to put the feeling of displeasure at the forefront." And so, we get an interpretation of the experience of anxiety that is clearly essential. Most authors put it at the forefront as an essential characteristic: "a painful uneasiness of mind" (Webster, 1956), "an unpleasant state of mind" (English and English, 1958) and "an unpleasant-feeling state, clearly distinguishable from other emotional states" (Ruebush, 1963).[2] Chapman puts it even stronger when he describes anxiety as "an emotional pain." (1967)

2 Characterisations taken from E.E. Levitt, 1968, pp. 25-26.

3. Different kinds of anxiety

In everyday life, people distinguish different kinds of anxiety but they are not all equally important in our study of fluctuating normal anxiety. Yet, it is helpful to mention them so that we can see which are important for our longitudinal study of socialised anxiety-driven reactions and which are not.

Momentary and sustained anxiety

Everybody is familiar with momentary, passing anxiety. We can read descriptions of it in every novel. They are the basic ingredient of many films. According to the circumstances, they can be quite mild or very intense. However, the reaction itself is very short-lived. What remains thereafter, the after-effect, can no longer be called anxiety or much less fear. Precisely because of the fact that it is so short, we should ask ourselves whether this is anxiety or fear. On the other hand, passing anxiety is important for the study of anxiety-induced behaviour. The main problem is to know how long anxiety has to be present to become socially noticeable, i.e., how long it takes before we see changes in behaviour that can be interpreted as being a reaction to it.

This brings us directly to long-lasting anxiety and the awareness of it. We can recognize momentary anxiety as such only when we become aware of it. If it does not reach consciousness, it is as if it had not existed. We cannot detect it by way of a defensive reaction as it is not triggered because of its brevity. Long-lasting anxiety can be noticeable by its intensity and then we become conscious of it.[3] However, it can also be latent, because it is either too feeble to reach consciousness or because it is repressed. In both cases, however, behaviour will make it possible for us to detect its presence owing to the fact that the duration causes behavioural attitudes and defensive reactions, which others can recognize as anxiety-driven reactions.

---

3 A relevant study of this was made by P.A. Sorokin, *Man and Society in Calamity. The Effect of War, Revolution, Famine, Pestilence upon the Human Mind, Behavior, Social Organization and Cultural Life.* (New York, 1942) It is remarkable that the word "anxiety" does not figure in the index and the word "fear" only in relation with war, on pp. 22-25.

The problem of "normal" levels of anxiety

Our study is confronted with another, quite fundamental problem: the distinction between normal anxiety, heightened anxiety, and exaggerated anxiety. Normal anxiety is less interesting to most researchers. It is measured on a scale and taken into account when one has to distinguish between normal and abnormal anxiety such as in neuroses. At that moment, we need "normal" anxiety as a reference point. It implicitly shows us that, for most researchers, the omnipresence of "a little" anxiety is normal. This is important when one wishes to study the evolution of normal anxiety, but what about the distinction between normal, heightened, and exaggerated anxiety.

The reason why we must assume the presence of normal anxiety is obvious. It does not reach our consciousness and is therefore nonexistent to us. Whether or not anxiety reaches consciousness could in fact serve as a dividing line between anxiety that is normal or no longer normal. This, however, is all but obvious. In psychology, unconscious anxiety has been a familiar — and accepted — fact since Freud pointed out that anxiety could be repressed. The mechanism of repression enables us to ban extreme anxiety from our consciousness; we are no longer aware of it. This, again, brings the dividing line between normal and no longer normal anxiety up for discussion. Anxiety not reaching consciousness because it is too weak seems rather obvious for normal fear. Yet, the mechanism of repression and the effort put in by mental energy can keep strong anxiety out of the reach of consciousness.

Nevertheless, the principle of normal anxiety being unconscious is tenable because of the permanent and massive presence of repressed intense anxiety. A pathological condition of society, so to speak, would prevent the greater part of society from functioning normally. In such a case, numerous cultural phenomena would have to be explained as symptoms of the massive repression of extreme anxiety.

We think we can assume that a kind of normal anxiety, an average anxiety level, is present in everyone.

If we assume now that this average level slowly rises and slowly falls, parallel to the long waves in economic matters, this implies that we cannot see this as an unchanging average level. That is why it is a mistake to speak of the absence of anxiety during periods of prosperity and the appearance of anxiety during periods of recession. Putting it like this would imply that there would also be a zero point.

Individual anxiety and forms of collective anxiety

The experience of anxiety is a strictly individual matter. We can speak of collective anxiety when a large section of the population is threatened by the same disaster; anxiety for the destruction of the environment, for example. In this case, we can speak of collective anxiety, as each member of the group knows that the others are anxious, too.

As in this case they know why they are anxious, the term "fear" might be more appropriate here. We can see forms of collective fear that are more direct, for example in cases of panic, when everybody can feel their neighbours' fear.

All these forms of fear share the characteristic that they are too brief to develop cultural instruments that help people to live with this fear.

Normal anxiety is yet another form of collective anxiety. The continuous presence of collective anxiety turns the means that different sections of the population use to cope with this anxiety into cultural instruments.

What part do internal factors play in this? External circumstances, for example? This will always remain an academic question. It is very difficult to estimate the part played by the facts from the first category as they are often mixed up with inner causes triggered by external circumstances.

Individual differences begin to play an important role when external anxiety-causing circumstances are less intense and do not elicit uniform reactions as much as in other cases. There is a greater margin for the individual dimension and the reaction to it, to the extent that external anxiety-inspiring circumstances are weaker. In this case, character, temperament, and other personality traits are given their chance. For example, if jogging, aerobics, and other forms of physical exercise have an alleviating influence on anxiety — and we may assume that due to the prolonged recession the average level of anxiety in society increases — the number of joggers in the streets may increase, because there are just a number of people with personality traits for which jogging is a more efficient anxiety-decreasing cultural instrument than for many others.

So, personality traits and social pressure make, so to speak, a selection of individuals in their search for the most efficient cultural instrument that can help to lessen anxiety.

The practical consequence of all this is that, when studying collective anxiety, we must bear in mind that individual traits are interrelated with the different forms of collective defence mechanism. We will elaborate on the other variables that play a role later.

Latent anxiety and its socio-cultural recognition

Acute forms of anxiety pose no problem; they are clearly recognizable. Latent anxiety is a different problem, because of its unconsciousness.[4] However, many forms of behaviour we find when we study acute forms of anxiety are not relevant to the study of lasting, latent normal anxiety. Latent normal anxiety is simply not characterized by the specific behaviour we find as a consequence of acute forms of anxiety.

In sociological studies we deal with behaviour of groups, with sections of a population, with masses. By definition, this behaviour reflects whole cultural manifestations. When we want to know what is going on in the minds of these masses, our only source is the cultural reflection of the behaviour of large sections of the population. It is the analysis of their cultural instruments that must enable us to say what is going on, or went on, in their minds.

Of course, we also have the possibility of investigating a few individuals and generalizing the results. This is made possible by the study of ego-sources. Unfortunately, in most cases, only elites produce that sort of source; the rest of society, especially the average person, has no part in it.

As a last resort, we can but ask which cultural instruments can be seen as means to lessen collective anxiety, in other words, to what extent these cultural instruments serve the function of lessening or averting anxiety for those who use them. Their appearance or disappearance, or the increase and decrease of their use, can be seen as symptomatic of the increase or decrease in the level of anxiety.

4 "The degree of awareness of a feeling does not indicate anything of its strength or importance. Concerning anxiety this means not only that we may have anxiety without knowing it, but that anxiety may be the determining factor in our lives without our being conscious of it," says K. Horney (1937, p. 40).

Anxiety, fear and the conversion of anxiety into fear

To avoid misconceptions, we want to come back to a distinction we mentioned earlier. The fact that we are dealing with "anxiety" must not tempt us to brush aside "fear" as being irrelevant. Sometimes it appears that fear is deeply rooted in anxiety, deeper that we would suspect at first sight. It often happens that fear can help us to detect anxiety or, in any case, to suspect its presence.

The conversion of anxiety into fear takes place simply as follows: people who, for a reason unknown to them, are anxious will, without being aware of it, try to find something to be afraid of. Thus, their anxiety finds an object and they will have something clearly recognizable that they can fear. "When anxiety occurs, the Ego tries to seek refuge in fear by searching for an object," says A. Kronfeld, in Freudian terms. (S. Vestdijk, 1968, p. 49)

Why does this happen? What incites the anxious person to search for an object? Simply because people are less oppressed by fear than by anxiety. Anxiety constricts, oppresses, and even paralyses, whereas one has the possibility to arm oneself against something one fears or one can flee, and the feeling of oppression disappears. The conversion of anxiety into fear is therefore a defence mechanism, which enables us to explain many cultural phenomena such as the increase of xenophobia and anti-Semitism. Which of course raises the question of the economic depression during periods in which xenophobia and anti-Semitism are — or were — rampant.

The notion of "free-floating anxiety" ("l'angoisse flottante," in French) that "is present in the background and can occasionally graft itself onto somatic symptoms or onto impressions," as Laplanche (1980, pp. 27-29) puts it, has to be put in this context. Because of the fact that anxiety has no object — that is to say not in the accounts of a number of authors — one should presume that anxiety is always free-floating, in search of something to fear. On the other hand, it strikes us that most of the authors who mention free-floating anxiety do not make any distinction between normal and pathological forms of anxiety. It would seem that there is a need for this and that there is only a variation in intensity so that the conversion of free-floating normal anxiety can follow a cultural course such as xenophobia or anti-Semitism, whereas the conversion of more intense forms of free-floating anxiety cannot be realized automatically but has to be brought about by therapy.

Variables in the experience of anxiety and its manifestations

It is obvious that the classic variables that influence human behaviour, such as class differences, age differences, differences of sex, and the differences in personality traits and character structure already mentioned before, have their influence on the way in which anxiety is experienced, on the way in which one is sensitive to it, and how one reacts.

As said before, an automatic selection of personality traits occurs when a choice of cultural instruments is made. Depending on the cultural instrument one analyses, the social groups concerned will show different social characteristics. While the symptoms of an increased presence of anxiety will be present in almost every group within society, the activities of very small groups can also contribute to shaping the view of society. Take the example of the number of terrorists. They may be few, but there is abundant evidence that there is a definite relation between the number of terrorist attacks and the economic situation. Considering this, we should ask ourselves how high the level of anxiety in society should rise to produce these small groups of terrorists.

4. Individual perception of anxiety

Now, if we want to construct a model of anxiety-driven behaviour, we have to define anxiety leaving out of account the eliminations we carried out before. We should consider brief, acute, pathological, and temporary anxiety only insofar it can help us to construct a model of permanent normal anxiety.

A displeasing state of tension

Anxiety causes tension that tries to find a solution, says Fröhlich. (1982, p. 208) We would like to go further and say that anxiety does not cause tension but *is* tension, and so it is one of the components of anxiety in itself. Levitt (1968, p. 33) argues that it can be seen as a state of unbalance, caused by a psychological need, leading to behaviour that tries to satisfy the need and thus restores the balance. This is a very valuable view: anxiety would prompt a certain kind of behaviour, namely the behaviour that should reduce inner tension. So a specific form of behaviour flows forth from anxiety, behaviour that would not have been present if anxiety would not have been present? What does that mean in the social sphere?

Increased involvement of the Ego

An even more important feature that helps us in our description of the feeling of anxiety is not the cause but the object of the anxiety, in the sense of what is being threatened. On this, most authors agree: "All causes of the feeling of anxiety have one thing in common: they threaten the feelings of self-esteem and self-confidence of the individual; they affect the individual's self-image of a competent and respected human being," says Chapman. (1976, p. 70) In this context, we would say that the Ego is threatened. The wholeness, the integrity of the individual, as it were, is threatened. This should not be seen as a purely causal connection. Van Raalten puts it very aptly in a metaphor: "Man can be anxious, but he *is* anxiety itself." (1981, p. 135)

If this is also correct for the masses, and in the supposition that the decreasing long wave increases insecurity and anxiety, we should see an increased involvement of the Ego in contemporary society. And this is undoubtedly the case, but it is not interpreted as a symptom of anxiety, but as a sudden increase of narcissism — with which it bears a resemblance, but only on the face of it. If it is true that during a decreasing long wave people present an as yet undeterminably increased level of anxiety, it implies that these people are more self-centred than in the preceding period of economic boom. We must picture this reorientation of thinking and emotional life towards the inside, towards themselves, as a structural change — if we may use the term here — of the whole mind and not simply as a change of course in their interest towards themselves. The whole Ego becomes Ego-centred.

However, it is necessary to be prudent with respect to the problem of people being self-centred. Humans are beings who are self-centred out of sheer necessity. Individualism, egocentrism, and so on, have always existed. In the case of egocentrism because of anxiety, however, we are dealing with a very specific form of egocentrism. It is not a curious or a sensual interest in oneself; it is the attention of a person with a toothache for his pain. There is no choice here of turning off egocentrism for a longer or a shorter time; one can but repress it or overcome it with more intense emotions.

Anxiety weakens the Ego and makes it hesitant

Whereas the non-anxious individual is in general full of self-confidence, i.e., whereas he sees himself as the legitimate just measure of things, the Ego of an anxious individual has partly or completely lost this certainty. Anxiety is precisely the state of mind, which — if it is present — affects the individual's identity and in particular his self-assurance.

The remarkable thing about this is that doubting oneself can function as an additional source of anxiety, i.e., one of the consequences of anxiety is an increase in the existing anxiety. It results in a further weakening of the Ego and a further increase in the concentration on oneself. (Van Raalten, 1981, p. 98)

However, how should we translate this into everyday behaviour? Probably as follows: the questions one is assailed with demand more time to reflect, cause more hesitation, and one makes room for seeking advice and obtaining more certainty. This also means that in certain cases people become more suggestible to prestigious and authoritative — or, as the case may be, authoritarian — arguments.

A good example to illustrate the functioning of the weakened Ego is the way one takes a decision. In times of self-assurance, i.e., in a period with a low level of anxiety, taking a decision is an Ego-affirming act; it strengthens the relatively self-satisfied Ego. Since we are in a period of economic boom, taking a decision also has positive consequences. In other words, in a period of economic boom, the number of decisions that turns out negatively is smaller than during a recession, not because of the quality of the decisions, of course, but because of the economic trend. In hierarchical situations, hierarchy is perceived as an obstruction, since final decisions always have to be moved up to a higher level of authority and one cannot "taste" the pleasure of one's own decisions and flatter one's Ego. During a period with a high level of anxiety, one is confronted with a much more hesitant Ego, which has more difficulty taking decisions. In fact, in such a period, moving up decisions to a higher level provides a kind of safeguard.

The more hesitant the Ego, the less eager it is to be confronted with moments at which it has to take decisions. This implies that people will to an increasing degree appreciate the rules and regulations concerning all matters that do not lead to misinterpretation by others — misinterpretations that would be less favourable in the eyes of the Ego.

Increased emotionality

The fourth essential characteristic of any feeling of anxiety — after the displeasing tension, increased egocentrism, and weakening of the Ego — is the increase of emotionality. This characteristic is quite a lot more difficult to explain than the previous ones.

Saying, *in everyday speech*, that people will react more emotionally under the influence of anxiety is quite clear. We mean to say that their reactions will be less well considered, more spontaneous, more impulsive. We mean to say that their behaviour will be less controlled by judgment. Thus, we set emotional behaviour against rational, well-considered behaviour, almost as an antithesis. This does not mean, however, that emotional behaviour would be incorrect. "Reacting emotionally" is often used as a synonym of "reacting in an uncontrolled way," by which we mean the control of the intellectual faculties. It is, as it were, falling back on the way in which one reacted as a small child when judgement and reasonable conduct were hardly achievable — a regression to earlier behavioural patterns.

There is a second meaning of emotionality in everyday life. We sometimes speak of a calm way of reasoning and an emotional way of reasoning, in which the word takes on the meaning of "emotionally charged." We can recognize its intensity by the intonation but also by the kind of arguments that are used, which derive from the emotions rather than from reason. In this meaning too, we may presume that reason has been pushed into the background.

Minor, everyday forms of anxiety do not show these indications with respect to increased emotionality — and what that emotionality implies — so clearly. The more intense these forms of anxiety become, the more they become evident; *in cases of disaster*, for example, of panic, in an emergency, and so on. In many cases, reason — or should we say realistic thinking — is lost, and people are driven only by anxiety-induced reflexes. When we call these intense forms of anxiety to mind, another characteristic appears that, without doubt, is present in milder, more latent forms of anxiety, namely the tendency to fall back on rather irrational and even magical/mythical ways of thinking.

There are quite a few experiences in everyday life in which linking the notion of anxiety and the notion of *magical/mythical ways of thinking* appears to be obvious. This is the case, for example, of the young man who takes a good-luck charm with him to an important exam. Broadly speaking it is the problem of the increase of faith and superstition in situations of increased anxiety. Every historian is familiar with periods beset by with disasters or infectious diseases when suddenly churches were crammed with people. It is easy to give a simplistic explanation. One could say that, obviously, when all rational — or rather realistic — solutions have failed, people appeal for paranormal or supernatural help. Well, that is not at all obvious. In the distant past, falling back on magical/mythical ways of thinking has determined human behaviour. By depicting animals, the hunters who lived in the caves of Lascaux hoped to have a better chance of "catching" them when they were hunting. In times of anxiety and emergency, many "modern" people, again, give these magical/mythical ways of thinking a stronger chance. Of course, in times of a decreasing long wave, the whole process of increasing emotionality does not take a clearly marked shape. What we see here is a rapid "emotionalisation" of the field of observation in everyday life. (Fröhlich, 1982, p. 240)

5. Characteristics of anxiety-driven behaviour

Anxiety is omnipresent, says K. Horney explicitly (1964, p. 22), and so are the defence mechanisms people develop against it. So we must assume that when angst — or Kierkegaard's "existential anxiety" — in society increases, compensation and defence mechanisms grow in importance in all individuals without them reaching their aim, namely permanently cutting down their increasing anxiety. They keep working at it, until they reach a subsequent phase of social development, so to speak.

The mechanisms that are intended to lessen the state of anxiety are of a very different nature and have dissimilar effects. The concrete question here is: what do people who are anxious experience? Sometimes, when people are extremely anxious, these experiences are clearly recognizable, whereas they are not so with basic anxiety or existential angst, which are constantly present in society and in all individuals.

Feelings of inferiority give occasion for the development of compensating needs for *self-aggrandizement* in order to impress oneself and others. This happens with extreme attention to outward appearance, display of wealth, possessions, antiques, travel, and so on, says Horney almost literally. (1964, pp. 33, 84 and ch. 10) One has to keep in mind, however, that seeking after these attributes does not really give satisfaction, but only lessens anxiety. Therefore, there is a never-ending urge — or compulsion — to keep going on with it. In the same respect, G. Condrau says that, today, money is no longer a means of exchange but a bearer of an unrelenting accumulation of wealth as a means to boost the Ego. (1962, p. 102) In other words, the compulsive accumulation of wealth as a therapeutic remedy against anxiety.

Exactly the opposite is *withdrawal*, with which Horney means: becoming independent of others (p. 85). Becoming independent of material needs can be achieved, as mentioned above, by accumulating wealth, but he who does so to lessen his anxiety will hardly risk touching this wealth and will try to stretch his wealth. To obtain the same effect, one can also do the opposite and try to limit one's needs to a minimum. Independence of inner needs can be attained by disengaging oneself emotionally from others, by containing emotions and emotional ties. One of the basic principles here is taking nothing seriously, not even oneself, which does not mean that one does not feel important. An attitude that is often found in intellectual circles, says Horney, cheekily. *Social anxiety* fits very well in this context.

Of course, anxiety has a fundamental effect on our attitude towards our *fellow beings*. People need their fellow beings to affirm themselves. Anxious people's fear consists of the fact that they cannot get this confirmation, which make the condition worse, as a result of which they will find it "safer" not to confront others and even avoid them. Which brings us to the paradoxical situation that, in phases in which one needs others more, communication with them becomes more difficult than in phases in which one needs others less, simply because one is less anxious.

Affection, however, can be obtained by yet other means, namely by *submission*. If gaining affection becomes so important that one's sense of security depends on it, one is only too ready to pay the price, which usually leads to a submission to the wishes of others. However, it often happens that a person is not capable of believing in any form of affection and then one's submissive attitude is not aimed at gaining affection but at gaining protection. It is clear that this can shed a different light on family life and more specifically on relations between men and women in periods of increased normal anxiety. (G. Condrau, 1962, p. 102)

Power and authority can be imposed and forced upon people but power and authority can also be created by *submission*. According to K. Horney, next to affection, power, and withdrawal, submission is one of four defence mechanisms against basic anxiety. Submission can come about in regard to people or institutions or neither of them. In the last case, the defence mechanism against normal anxiety takes the shape of submission to certain traditional or standardized norms, or to the rites of a religion, or to the desires of one or other domineering personality. The latter is a very important mechanism since it is assumed that power and authority are imposed and maintained by some corresponding method of coercion — or compulsion. Countless studies of fascist regimes or authoritarian forms of government ignore the fact that there can be something like a demand and even a need for submission as a defence mechanism and thus a reestablishment of inner balance, with a positive effect on people's minds. Butullo describes a characteristic of this defence mechanism against anxiety: fatalism, which reinforces this tendency to submission. Butullo postulates that fatalism — a kind of inner acceptance of the course of events — is closely followed by a feeling of security. In rational terms, it is a feeling of respect for the mystery and the eternity of existence. (1984, p. 53)

Obviously, striving for *power*, possessions, and prestige are very important as defence mechanisms against anxiety. Horney devotes a whole chapter to it. However, we wonder to what extent she is correct when she concludes that neither Adler or Freud recognized the role of anxiety in causing this striving for power. After all, the feeling of inferiority which is at the centre of Alfred Adler's theory can be seen as the cause of anxiety and insecurity and many behaviours developed to compensate this feeling of inferiority, such as striving for power, can be seen as serving as defence mechanisms. A study of Adler from this point of view would certainly refine our understanding of anxiety-driven behaviour.[5]

It may be useful to point out that, obviously, not every striving for power is a defence mechanism against anxiety. It can equally well proceed from a sound spirit of competition or the will to change things or to show one's strength and so many other reasons. It is just so that in these last cases it gives much more satisfaction, which is not the case with striving for power as a defence against anxiety. All in all, it is a question of degree and we will never be able to draw precise lines.

The structure of power will also be different depending on whether people themselves are anxious or not. If they are, they will welcome this striving in others as it enables them to satisfy their deep-down longing to transfer responsibility to others. Angst with regard to freedom — a notion Erich

5 In his introduction to A. Adler, *Lebenskenntnis* (Frankfurt am Main, 1978), W. Metzger writes that since the publication of his writings on the doctor as educator in 1904, Adler was convinced that combating anxiety and inspiring courage were some of the fundamental duties of the educator.

Fromm made world-famous — has to be viewed in this context.[6] We do strive for freedom of choice as long as we lack it but as soon as we are given the freedom, we shy away from decisions. The more options and freedom we have, the worse.

It goes without saying that many more factors play a decisive role in this issue, such as the current pressure to conform, the degree of social control, the formation of habits, and so on, just as they do indeed in every experience of anxiety and in every avoidance of it. But it seems obvious that an increase in the insecurity of the Ego will exert a decisive influence on the attitude of many with regard to the problem of the desired and the pursued — or not pursued—measure of freedom one wants to attain.

Making anxiety subconscious, suppressing it, is a defence mechanism against anxiety.

However, we must not forget that suppression requires a lot of energy. Horney calls it *narcotising*, a term no other psychologist uses in this meaning but is extremely useful. (1964, p. 33) Narcotising can be achieved consciously by using alcohol and drugs and also tranquillisers, of which a much greater range is now available than Horney's time: just look at the worldwide success of Prozac today. Another way to narcotise anxiety is by seeking oblivion, in one's work, for example. It is recognizable by its compulsive character and by the feeling of discomfort that appears on Sundays and during holidays. Becoming engrossed in social work for fear of being alone is another form of narcotising anxiety. In this case, it is not so important whether one is conscious of anxiety as a driving force rather than as a vague feeling of discomfort or uneasiness — a malaise.

A characteristic of anxiety-driven behaviour that we do not straightforwardly see in society and in culture is a *permanent alertness*, an unrelenting watchfulness, which is typical for anxious people who want to be ready for the dangers looming in every corner. This would indicate that anxious people always try to keep well informed about what is going on in the world and hence read several newspapers and in so doing, are especially

6 Erich Fromm, *Escape from Freedom* (New York, 1941). In chapter 5, Fromm distinguishes between escape from authoritarianism, escape into destruction, and escape into conformism.

receptive to all threatening information. In fact, it also implies that anxious people have a relation with *the future and the past* that is different from non-anxious people. A non-anxious person sees only a non-threatening future and for the rest does not worry too much whereas for the anxious person future developments are an endless source of worry.

4. Behavioural functionalism as an observation method and the first step towards an explanation

Functionalism — structural functionalism most certainly — has been an important school in sociology. In the eighties, however, functionalism passed into disuse. This is most regrettable, while functionalism is a school of thought that does not fit the models of ordinary causal thinking. We want to reinstate functionalist thinking as scientific method. Functionalist thinking does this in a specific manner: instead of confining itself to exploring the relation between individual behaviour and social structures, functionalism explores the relation between the behaviour of individuals and groups and the needs inciting them to proceed with this behaviour.

The conversion of traditional functionalism into "behavioural functionalism" compels us to take a different view when observing and describing behaviour. It also compels us to review the strict division between the different social science disciplines and to re-evaluate the psychological side of sociological, political, historical and other interpretations. It also means that behavioural functionalism confronts us with the lack of understanding and the inadequacy of many such interpretations, which must urge us to remain modest.

1. A double dichotomy

It is in all respects an odd thing to see how people time and again succeed in carrying through such fundamental dichotomies in their observations, as if they were Iron Curtains.

The separation of reasoning and emotion goes far back into our history and has found many symbolic forms of expression there. The rational has been put on the same footing as the divine, purity, the light. Emotion was instinctive, it was bestial, and it was darkness.

All this might be indifferent to us were it not that we are trying to find out the how and why of human behaviour and, as a consequence, the important part the psyche plays in this.

Everyday reality shows us the unity of reason and emotion. We can observe both at work in our own behaviour. The practice of psychology confirms it every day. However, many people still find the unison of rationality and emotion in the epistemology of social sciences to be an inappropriate joke.

It was Emile Durkheim who, at the end of the 19th century, built this dichotomy into sociology and proclaimed it the fundamental dogma of sociology.[1] For Durkheim, any interpretation of a social phenomenon by a psychological phenomenon was a false interpretation. The causes and function of social phenomena should be sought in other social realities. Social phenomena should not be reduced to other disciplines.

In this way, Durkheim gave future generations of sociologists free play to disregard psychology. Durkheim's sophistic reasoning is quite simple: the whole presents us with characteristics that are not present in the components, which does not exactly mean that the sum is more than the parts. "The hardness of bronze does not lie in the copper or in the tin or in the lead of which it is composed, which are soft, pliable elements; the hardness lies in their mixture." Following on this example with a perfect analogy, he then states: "Let us apply this example to sociology. If you agree with me that the synthesis *sui generis* of which every society consists brings forth new phenomena, different from those which appear in the consciousness of the individual, we must accept that the specific phenomena are implicit in the society that brings them forth and not in its parts, i.e. its members."

This quotation of Durkheim's words brings us right into the middle of the second dichotomy, the break-up of the unity between the individual and the group.

It is clear that the study of groups has to reckon with the many features and qualities that people have in common, without at all detracting from the

1 Emile Durkheim, *Les Règles de la méthode sociologique* (Paris, 1895)

meaning and values of individual differences. To put it in an image: if a film, a pop song, et cetera, are appreciated from Chicago to Tokyo, then people have something in common. The communality of cultural consumption and, more generally, of needs, implies a communality of the predisposition to appreciate cultural expressions. The analysis of consumption, and the analysis of needs, automatically leads us to a communality of needs.

2. Functionality and behavioural functionalism

Now that we have the word "need," we can also introduce "functionality." Generally, there is a need to perform a particular action. An answer is given to the need, namely the action itself — the action that revealed the conjecture of the existence of the need. The answer is given, or rather, the action is performed in order to remove or diminish the original need. After a longer or shorter period, the need may appear again, in the same or in an altered form.

Let us now propose a new linguistic convention, a new semantic operation; let us call "functional" the extent to which behaviour itself cancels out the underlying need — which, more often than not, we do not fully know.

This functionality of the behaviour of individuals, groups and masses with respect to their underlying needs, at the moment when these actions are performed, we will call "behavioural functionalism".

Behavioural functionalism is a way in which we look at people and their behaviour, as well as the first step towards a scientific method for describing it; a method that is different from the current one. The elements of which this method is composed are by no means new. On the other hand, in our view, their synthesis is original. It may ultimately offer the prospect of formulating hypotheses that are quite new.

Behavioural functionalism assumes that all human behaviour is an answer to underlying needs. In other words, whatever people do, from a behavioural functionalist viewpoint we must assume that a need precedes behaviour.

The underlying needs lead people to perform actions that, in the first place, aim to answer those needs as best as possible within a given context. We use the word "needs" here in a variant sense, as a sort of collective term to categorize needs that cannot yet be defined. That is how we postulate "the need to go to the cinema." Only by further research can we define the nature of the need. In other words, we do not know the need but since the person goes to the cinema, the need must be there.

Now the next step. For the spectator, seeing a film is a very specific experience, which is in the first place psychological. If the spectator is pleased, we may assume that the experience of seeing the film has lessened, or cancelled, the original need that incited him or her to go to the cinema, until he or she takes a fancy to go to the cinema again. As we have already said, we do not know the original need that urged the person to go to the cinema but the analysis of the film the person saw may perhaps tell us more about the nature of that need.

In brief, we can say that when a person performs an action or acts in a certain way, a need lies at the basis of this behaviour. The behaviour he shows has a definite effect on him or her and this effect is what people seek. It is what completely or partly fulfils the original need. More briefly: need A leads to behaviour B, which has effect C, and this effect C cancels out need A for a longer or a shorter time.

This outline enables us to define the concepts of function and functionality in a noticeably variant way. Behaviour B is functional to the extent that effect C cancels the original need A. Therefore, the essence of behavioural functionalism is psychological. However, as soon as we examine the origin of need A, as to its nature and intensity, we find ourselves in society. When we research the nature and sorts of behaviour that are possible in an historical context, we find ourselves in society once more. Again, when we ask ourselves if it were possible to find alternative behavioural patterns that might meet the needs in a different way. From the behavioural functionalist point of view, the notion of "functional alternatives" is used in this sense only.

The behavioural functionalist angle also offers an onset of an explanation. Indeed, after a first descriptive phase of many, often disconnected, behaviours and needs, there is the question of a model, a theory, that might explain this multiplicity of behaviour and thus of needs. A theory that we will need to explain in psychological terms.

For the elaboration of this theory we base ourselves on a battery of behaviours — i.e. fulfilled needs — which are at first sight rather heterogeneous and even incoherent. One can, for example, come to the conclusion that, in a given period, emotionalism in society has increased since we can observe it in political attitudes, in artistic productions, in the style of film productions, in the argumentation of marketing and so on. However, once we have detected this increased emotionality we can extrapolate it into areas that had not been included in the survey. This is precisely the value of a theory, of a model. It even allows us to make extrapolations into a near future.

3. "Needs" as the basic idea in behavioural functionalism

First, we must regret the fact that the — rather extensive — literature on needs lacks references to the notions of function and functionality. Conversely, we see that most books on functionalism do not mention needs. In our conception of functionalism, the two are inextricably bound together.

We also see that in literature there is total confusion about who or what can have needs and what one can need.

Of course, the notion of "need" is not new. No more than the notion of "functionality." We use it in most disciplines, in different degrees of concreteness or abstraction. It is mostly used — except in psychology — as a metaphor but often also as a collective term for the needs of large groups of individuals. There is the need for capital, the need for love, the need for information, the need for vitamin A, the need for doctors, the need for protection, the need for tractors, there are medical and social needs, true and false needs, religious needs, major and minor needs, the need for modern languages and so on. There are the needs of the market, the needs of agriculture, the needs of neurotics, of youngsters and adults, the needs of the population, the needs of the minorities, the families, the economy, the essential needs — or necessities — of life... An endless list of needs.[2]

At this point, again, we propose a semantic operation, a linguistic convention. Let us consider everything that incites people to perform acts as an answer to the underlying need to perform these acts. Let us also

2 "Perhaps the most challenging — and still unsolved problem — of needs is how to define a need." (K. Lederer, *Human Needs. A contribution to the Current Debate*, p. 3.)

consider that the causes and the contextual factors that generate these needs are not known *a priori*.

Neither does this linguistic convention imply that behaviour triggered by these needs can fully satisfy them. Nor does our linguistic convention say whether this satisfaction is more or less definitive.

The reason why we present this as a linguistic problem — and how we see this — is intended to reject all references to existing theories — including the theory of needs itself — as unsuitable. We use the word "needs" only as an operational notion, without references to systems of value, ideologies, or world and social views in any shape, manner or form.

On the face of it, the result of this operation may seem very limited. Let us look at a range of various behaviours: saving, going to the cinema, having sex, setting out on a journey, mowing the lawn, reading the newspaper, wearing a red or a brown coat, not wanting to wear a hat, reading poetry, dancing, celebrating carnival, going to Mass, hanging framed pictures on the wall of the living room, gossiping, swapping jokes, and so on. The choice of these behaviours does not exactly show a clearly recognizable underlying material obligation or need. Let us now call it a series of twenty needs instead of a series of twenty behaviours: the need to save, the need to go to the cinema, the need to mow the lawn, and so on. We must now explain the origin of twenty exactly-defined needs instead of a series of twenty behaviours. It steers our thought in quite a different direction.

Looking at it more closely, this operation led us to a number of fundamental changes. The actions in themselves are facts of a sociological nature; the need to perform certain acts is psychological. Concrete everyday behaviour inextricably binds them together; there is no need to distinguish between the two in order to act efficiently. In this light, Durkheim's Iron Curtain dividing them seems very artificial.

Approaching behaviour from underlying needs, we arrive at a description of the reality of a variety of behaviours as a variety of needs: the need to go to the cinema, the need to travel, and so on. However, by raising behaviour from the sociological to the psychological level, we get an answer to the question "why" as well: why does one have the need to save, why does one have the need to travel, why do so few people feel the need to wear a hat in winter, or — as N. Elias said:[3] why do people feel the need to lick the fat from their fingers; it goes to their stomach anyway...

If we want to answer those questions, we need an alternative methodology.

4. The origin of needs

The nature and origin of needs is a problem that becomes important afterwards, after they have become known. No origin is excluded *a priori* and we must a priori assume that they can be manifold. They can be occasioned by the material context in which people find themselves, in general, i.e., their economical condition, as well as the particular reflection of it on their neighbourhood and their families. They may be of a genetic nature. They may be social, caused by relational and communicational structures, by their reading or group behaviour. Personality traits and the mental functioning that is characteristic of certain personality structures may cause them. They may be caused by long-lasting or momentary occurrences. They may be the result of over-adjustment, of indoctrination, of advertising, and so on.

Therefore, it is externally perceptible behaviour that refers to the existence of a need, or more correctly, that leads us to assume the presence of a need. That is why behavioural functionalism is, in the first place, descriptive and not explanatory. The description remains valid; the explanation may change.

5. Whose needs? Individual and social behaviour

By definition, behavioural functionalism is a method that does in the first place study the needs of individuals and not of groups. Functionalism is a method that first studies behaviour and reactions of people in order to recognize the needs. Ultimately, however, no social scientist is interested in the behaviour of individuals.

3 N. Elias, *Über den Prozess der Zivilisation* (1939). Elias describes which global social processes must take place from a certain moment in history so that people begin to find it disgusting to have fat on their fingers while eating.

How can we reconcile this with the notion of social phenomena? The opera, tourism, strikes, party conferences, the parliament, the family, the State, and so forth, are all social phenomena; not people. How can we avoid the pitfalls of methodological individualism?

It is our aim to develop behavioural functionalism into a research method for the study of social phenomena. We leave the study of what we would describe as strictly individual behaviour to the psychologists. However, with regard to the behaviour of individuals, we can ask the question of which behaviour is individual and which is social. A rather superfluous question, in our view, as no behaviour is purely individual, no more than any behaviour is exclusively social.

Nor is there any behaviour that is strictly individual, in the sense that it would not largely be shaped by a social context. Individual differences can be nothing more than differences in degree. If we ever found one-off behaviour in individuals, or rather, if the psyche of certain people were to function better with the awareness of the existence of one-of-a-kind behaviour (the need for one-off behaviour as a social phenomenon), then this so-called one-off behaviour must by definition be excluded from the field of social sciences.

Yet we are now confronted with a linguistic problem that has far-reaching consequences. The question of function can be — and often is — asked in two different ways, which we must keep apart. One question asks about an attitude, the other about people's behaviour. One can ask questions about the function of behaviour and one can ask questions about the function of a social phenomenon, as in structural functionalism. To put it concretely: what is the function of going to a museum, or, what is the function of a museum; what is the function of reading edifying novels, or, what is the function of literature; and so on.

Generally speaking, we can say that the question of the function of a social phenomenon itself almost automatically raises the question of the systems, of the macro-sociological structures, in which these social phenomena could be functional. With firm conviction Alvin Gouldner put it like this: 'The intellectual fundament of functional theory in sociology is the concept of a 'system.' Functionalism is nothing if it is not the analysis of social patterns as part of larger systems of behavior and belief." (1967, p. 141)

6. The experiential value of behaviour and the functioning of behavioural functionalism

The consequence of a social phenomenon or, rather, the consequence of participating in or the use of a social phenomenon is the most difficult point of behavioural functionalism but also the core of the whole system, in theory as well as in practice.

The first step towards a more precise knowledge of the functions of a social phenomenon is a more precise description of the overall circumstances in which the phenomenon "functions," making due allowance for the greatest possible completeness.

The second step, of course, is the description of the functionalist behaviour itself. As we have already said, this sets specific problems when we are dealing with a rather "impassive" participation in the functional phenomenon such as, for example, seeing a film. In this case, the analysis of the functional phenomenon itself — the film — remains the only possibility of gaining insight into what may come to the spectator's mind. Such an analysis is not always possible without a certain conjecture about the psychological processes that do play an important role when participating in a social phenomenon and should play an important role in making it functional. In the example of the film, the identification of the spectator with what happens on the screen plays an essential role. Without this identification, it would be impossible to "enjoy" it and the participation would not "function."

If we behave in a certain way, on account of a particular need, seeing a football match, for example, or mowing the lawn, or following a diet, it is this behaviour which — for a shorter or a longer period of time — cancels out or lessens the underlying need. The question we are confronted with is why, in what manner, behaviour can cancel out or lessen a need. To answer this question we must introduce a new and central notion we have not needed until now: the experiential value of behaviour.[4] A notion that comes

4 In his dictionary of psychology, A. S. Reber makes an amusing observation on the notion of "experience": "Basically, this term is used in the same sense in psychology as in everyday life. [...] This [...] does not mean that a confusion of ideas would not be possible. The confusion can arise because some will use the term exclusively to refer to physical facts whereas contemporary cognitivists also include 'occurrences in the head.' Should we include in these experiences the pink elephants an alcoholic sees or not?"

very close to it but which we do not retain because of certain connotations is the "practical value". Its role and meaning are so obvious that it is incomprehensible that such an essential notion so rarely appears explicitly — but all the more implicitly — in the explanations of behaviour.[5]

What we mean, very simply, in non-technical terms, is the effect of behaviour on the mind and the heart. Watching a football match, voting for an extremist party, saving, being active in a faction, starting up a new company, managing a company, seeing a western in a cinema, and so on, have a certain subjective effect on the people concerned which brought about by these behaviours. We propose to call it the experiential value. In other words, we observe the world in the light of its functional value.

The leap from the individual to the group is a smooth one. I want to listen to Pavarotti because it gives me a particularly pleasant feeling. In the stadium, I find that thousands of others have the same need. Who is sitting there then? A collectivity of seventy thousand individuals such as I? One collective need or seventy thousand needs? I want to do something useful for peace and in the peace movement I find thousands of others who have the same feeling. Same questions.

5 An attempt in this direction was made by Gerhard Schulze, *Die Erlebnisgesellschaft, Kultursoziologie der Gegenwart* (1992). He finds that in the past practical value — useful life, technical perfection, and usefulness — stood at the centre of the representation of products. Nowadays, the consumer stresses the 'Erlebniswert [*experiential value*] der Produkte' rather than its practical value. As it turns out, this 'Erlebniswert' appears to be a sort of 'aestheticising.' However, the meaning of this aesthetic experience remains unclear. The aesthetic experience, too, is a complex psychological experience. Schulz proves to be an obstinate sociologist. His work aims — as he himself says — to be in keeping with traditional sociological analysis. He accepts collective constructions such as intersubjective patterns not only in the field of actions but also of thinking and feeling and only these are fit for description. " [...] Über den hermetischen Bereich strikt individueller Subjektivität lässt sich wenig mehr sagen, als das es existiert." ["It is hard to say anything more about the hermetic range of strictly individual subjectivity than that it exists."] Again, Durkheim's Iron Curtain.

7. Functional alternatives

So we argue that a need lies behind every conduct and that this behaviour itself is an answer to that need. However, since we assume that the nature of the underlying need is indefinite, we do not know to what extent this behaviour cancels out the underlying need. In other words, this elimination or lessening can also be partial and only temporary. When the need returns, when the balance is upset again, the wish to repeat the behaviour that cancels out or lessens the need will arise again.

The "functional alternatives," i.e., the conduct of a different nature that will again be functional with respect to the underlying need, are important facts in our analysis of functionalism.

Apart from the question whether the individual is aware of having made a choice, the notion of functional alternatives presents us with the problem of options. This choice is important too. Indeed, it indicates that of all behaviour that is possible in the everyday context of the individual at a particular moment, the action that is performed is the one he "sees" to be most functional with respect to the underlying needs.

Not choosing alternative actions that are at one's disposal may also give us information for our research. We could compare it with the use of language. When someone uses a word, the listener knows what other words that are close at hand the speaker could have chosen and that the choice of the word that is used excludes the meanings of the other words that were not chosen.

This mode of thought gives a new dimension to our view of people's behaviour. Different forms of behaviour are not a purpose in themselves; they are only instruments, or means, to express knowledge of the experiential value of these forms of behaviour.

8. The experiential value of desire

If our needs lead us to performing certain acts, it is clearly with the prospect, with the desire to live a particular experiential value. We do not always know beforehand if the underlying need will be effectively satisfied; we can only know it afterwards, or we can, to a certain extent, expect it if we are already familiar with the behaviour and its effects.

In other words, what is the experiential value of desire? Of the desire that never must be realized, that is. It must not be realized because if the object of the desire were attained, one would lose the experiential value of the desire. Pursuing a utopia means that one can spend a whole life longing for it. For some, the experiential value of this longing is greater than the experiential value of attaining the utopia.

9. Behavioural functionalism and cultural dynamics

So, we have seen that all the behaviour people display should be seen as an answer to an underlying need. The notion of "need" designates all possible reasons and motivations that prompt people to display a particular behaviour: reasons and motivations that are known and unknown, conscious and subconscious, character-linked, momentary and prolonged, acute and barely compulsory, and so on. Initially, we should consider the origin and the nature of underlying needs to be unknown.

We have seen that behaviour is called functional to the extent that it satisfies (i.e. lessens or cancels) the underlying needs. With the exception of behaviour that is caused under external pressure, we have to consider all behaviour as functional. To what extent these behavioural patterns cancel out or lessen underlying needs, i.e., to what extent they are functional, should also be considered to be unknown.

We have also seen that social phenomena (a newspaper, an ideology, going to the opera, floral-patterned dresses...) continue to exist because of the individuals who take part in them or use them. Being or taking part in or making use of a social phenomenon has an effect on the individuals that is psychological before all else: it is the experiential value. This effect, or experiential value, is expected to cancel out or lessen the underlying needs that have motivated the individuals to take part in or use the social phenomena.

We have seen that the nature of the needs can only be known by means of the analysis of this psychological effect, the experiential value. Social phenomena that continue to exist because of the activities (behaviour) of individuals should be seen as functional on the grounds of the needs of the many individuals who maintain these social phenomena by their activities. The existence of social phenomena should therefore be seen as proof, not of an identity but of the similarity of the needs of many.

Hence, the evolution of social phenomena — cultural dynamics — reflects the evolution of the structure of the needs of its participants or users within the developing material, mental, and social context.

5. Construction of the long wave of anxiety

The hypotheses formulated in the preceding pages have put us in a very different situation. In the first chapter, we have seen that there are — to put it mildly — serious problems with following in the footsteps of the economists and giving a purely economic explanation of the turning points of the long wave as we know it from Kondratiev. To put it as Joseph Schumpeter did: there are "animal spirits" at work.

If we scan two centuries of European history with the scanner of the long wave, it appears that a certain number of cultural-historical and mental changes show the same cyclic course as Kondratiev's long wave. Not all of them can be as easily followed back to fluctuations in the market. Looking at the non-economic evolution of the last two centuries, we see certain currents becoming dominant and then subsiding. On the face of it, these currents indicate an increase and decrease in the level of anxiety in society, with peaks and low points that correspond with the peaks and lows of Kondratiev's long waves.

In order to pursue that question, chapter two went more deeply into the phenomenon of anxiety. We examined it not as a pathological state but as a mass phenomenon that has not become conscious. In other words, we were forced to postulate a certain feeling of insecurity, a certain basic anxiety — as Karen Horney puts it — which is constantly present in society, and is characterized — as we will see hereafter — by a certain cyclic evolution that bears a strong resemblance to the long waves of Kondratiev.

To examine this further, we were bound to reflect on the collective unconscious and its manifestation in the behaviour of a multitude of individuals. For this purpose, we have expanded on behavioural functionalism in the third chapter. This has enabled us to assume that overt behaviour can be, to a large extent, an expression of or an answer to deep-seated needs. The structure of deep-seated needs we are interested in here is the basic anxiety we find in masses. By means of behavioural functionalism and through our knowledge of the phenomenon of anxiety, we should be able to detect of a wave, or a cycle, of anxiety, which is no longer Kondratiev's cycle of prices.

The main question here is: which overt human behaviour will we use to detect the changes in the unconscious structure of needs, and more precisely the evolution of the anxiety that is present in the subconscious. This poses a heuristic problem: which sources can we find that enable us to study these changes over an effectively prolonged period and, even more importantly, to what extent can we use these sources as functional behavioural indicators for measuring and quantifying the evolution of deep-seated anxiety? Not until these conditions were met with, could we go further and substitute Kondratiev for these indicators, in the period for which Kondratiev's sources are available.

1. Fashion as a method

It may sound strange, but the best documented mass phenomenon that appears to be the subtlest indicator of the collective unconscious in our Western world is fashion, and more specifically women's fashion. This may seem strange at first sight, but on closer inspection it is not; quite the reverse.

Fashion has everything to do with people's behaviour, not just with opinions or views that are easy to register, but also with the emotional charge in these opinions and convictions that is usually indefinable. Wearing a dress of a particular colour, with a particular tailoring, and a specific design, is one of the most direct forms of womanly expression. Obviously, deciding on a particular dress always comes down to a choice, like the choice of a beautiful painting, or a nice home, or the choice of anything one likes. Thus, we could use many cultural products that have been, at a specific point in the past, the result of a selection by a specific group of people or by the masses, as an indicator of underlying feelings. Fashion however has an important additional element: it is a selection made by an individual, with which the individual significantly defines his identity, with respect to himself and with regard to the others, with the people around him or her. Dresses are worn; one puts them on. One is not oneself as a result of one's clothing alone, but it does play a major part. This implies a strong emotional bond between the individual and his clothing, as a result of which fashion serves in the first place as an emotional exteriorisation. Obviously, no one individual can wear just everything. Just like the subconscious urge to distinguish oneself, the subconscious urge to conform remains. In other words, one does not want to disagree too much with the norm, but then again one does not want to agree with it too closely either. This mechanism is not always as strictly present in all periods of the past. These and other social-psychological mechanisms inherent in our culture remain in full force when any individual choices are being made and thus also when selecting a particular dress of a particular colour and particular tailoring and design.

The enormous advantage is that fashion is a phenomenon that touches everyone — and that this has definitely been true since the middle of the 20th century. Most cultural behaviour that we know and which would be qualified for determining underlying anxiety has the drawback that only limited groups of society take part in it, so that we can never say whether the study of the results of this behaviour also apply to all others who do not participate in it. Fashion is a social phenomenon in which everyone is involved. Therefore it is obvious that we will leave haute couture, which concerns only a fraction of a percent of the population, out of consideration.

One could argue that a study of women's fashion leaves men out of the picture, which would call for a study of men's fashion. Such an objection passes over the fact that the dresses women choose and through which they exteriorise their identity are also set to a considerable extent to define their appearance and impression on men. In other words: in women's choices, men are positively, if not physically, present.

As a matter of fact, we did analyse men's fashion too, when we began with our study, and we came to the conclusion that men's fashion is governed by codes to a much larger extent than women's fashion, and that there is a greater urge to conform, as a result of which the fluctuations are less pronounced.

There is a final argument that makes it important to choose fashion as a source for our study of the underlying emotions of the masses: this source will remain available in the future; individuals will always have the tendency to express their identity by it.

Materially, we have based ourselves on the widely read Belgian women's magazines *Het Rijk der Vrouw*, *Libelle* and *Flair*, and registered the characteristics of 7,470 summer dresses. In 2000, the circulation of *Libelle/Het Rijk der Vrouw* was 214,700 copies and *Flair* 126,300. As these mass media are consumer products, we may assume that they reflect the prevailing taste. The law of averages eliminates occasional errors of judgment by the editors concerning the taste of the masses. Imposing taste — which may be possible in the case of haute couture — would surely not have been a profitable strategy for magazines that depend on sales and thus on the market.

2. Three main categories of analysis

Examining the three main categories that we have to distinguish when analysing fashion, it becomes clear that fashion is anything but only fashion. Therefore, we will distinguish three main categories: colour, tailoring, and design or pattern.

Without doubt, the first and most important characteristic is colour. A researcher who took the relationship between the preference for a colour and the underlying feelings of the individual the furthest is the Swiss professor Max Lüscher. He even went as far as trying to determine individuals' personality traits on the basis of successive colour preferences. His colour test became a bestseller in the United States in 1969 and in Great Britain, Germany, and Holland in 1971. Leaving aside the point of knowing to what extent Lüscher succeeded in this, the fact that he stresses the connection between colour and feelings is sufficient for us. Then again, we do not need academic studies to accept that people who are anxious and people who are feeling well and carefree will choose different preferred colours. As they are connected with different mechanisms of psychological development, which have nothing to do with the perception of this social situation, we leave the colour preferences of children out of it.

The second category is tailoring. Are the dresses long or short, do they have sleeves or not, is the waistline accentuated or not, is there a low neck or not... Any non-professional will understand that a women who wears an extremely short yellow or orange dress, without décolleté, without emphasis of the waist, what the French call a *robe sac*, feels differently from a woman of the same age who, on other days, and even in the middle of summer, chooses a grey or black dress that reaches below the knee or even lower — and thus hides her legs — with a marked waistline — and thus accentuates her hips — and a plunging décolleté — which emphasizes her bosom. One really need not have read Freud to suspect that we are confronted here with different representations of sexuality. What does the woman with the yellow dress want to express? What does the woman with the black dress show and what does she want to hide? It is obvious that both psychological configurations, both self-images that are expressed, give shape in a fundamental way to different relations with their partner or any other person. In the end, it would be surprising if deep-felt uncertainty and existential anxiety had not influenced the choice. The question is: what else can we infer from all this? Cultural psychologists can undoubtedly gain even more insight, but we do not intend to explore that field. For our purpose, it will be sufficient to register the evolution of the existential insecurity.

The patterns too — the print or design of the fabrics — will prove to be significant. There are periods with predominantly plain dresses, periods with round or floral patterns, or periods with stripes, checks, or other angular patterns. The study of the perception of these characteristics, which borders on applied aesthetics, could for example be carried through on the basis of the logos of trading names and companies. However, no anthologies of these to which me might refer seem to exist. Angles, stripes, checks and the like are incompatible with yellow dresses. It seems not to be done, aesthetically. Here too there is ample material for other branches of research.

3. A system of blind correlations

As early as 1992, we set out to make a longitudinal curve of all these fashion characteristics of the period 1946-1988 and to analyse the correlation between them. Next, we extended the period to 1956-2000, almost half a century. The hard statistical work that has since been done on this material has not induced us to change our method.

At that time, our study aimed to identify the system behind the evolution of fashion in the first place. The similitude with the long wave emerged only at the end and has not been explored further as at the time this question had not fully arisen.

In our 1992 study, we had come to the conclusion that certain colours, certain forms, and certain designs taken together were forming four sets of characteristics. That was a remarkable finding in itself, since it meant, in fact, that we could distinguish four types of women or, more correctly, four metamorphoses of women in half a century. For this purpose, we examined the correlation between all the characteristics of the 2,520 dresses from 1946 to 1988. We regrouped the characteristics that showed a strong correlation. Of course, not every characteristic showed an equally strong correlation with the cluster, but then again we could not have expected it. Some characteristics with a weaker correlation could even have been classified under a different cluster without disrupting the basic categories. When we extended the period to include 1956-2000, our earlier results hardly changed.

The analysis of the correlations shows that in a period of about one generation, from 1968-70 until 1990-92, i.e., not quite a half Kondratiev, the four types of dresses dominate in succession. In other words, as the years go by, the self-expression of women gradually changes into four successive identities, which can be precisely determined by statistical data. The type that dominates at the top of the long wave — around 1968-70 — is a woman who prefers to express herself through the colours yellow and orange, that is bright colours, and a short, sleeveless dress with round motifs. Barely a quarter of a century later, she, just like her daughters, expresses herself through a long, plain black dress without motifs or low neck. Between the lively and high-spirited crest and the sombre bottom with a high level of anxiety and uncertainty, we can still see two successive types, the first of which follows the yellow/orange crest and is no longer emotionally related to it and is characterized by the colour brown. As we proceed in time, this is followed by the blue/green type, again with its own characteristics, which are not related to the following black type. The type

Table 5.1: The four successive fashion clusters, 1956 - 2000

orange-yellow cluster	Pearson correlation	black cluster	Pearson correlation
yellow	.59	black	.70
orange	.44	grey	.18
red	.09	dark colours	.66
bright vivid colours	.57	unpatterned	.52
with patterns	.17	low neckline	.52
round patterns: mainly flower-patterned	.48	skirt length: maxi	.40
skirt length: mini	.58	stripes	.06
sleeveless	.47		
no emphasized waistline	.28		

brown cluster	Pearson correlation	blue-green cluster	Pearson correlation
brown	.47	blue	.44
violet	.07	green	.43
white	-.05	bright vivid colours	.57
pastel shades	.41	dots	.36
angular patterns: mainly checks	.27	skirt length: knee	.42
skirt length: calf	.55	high neckline	.35
with sleeves	.66		
emphasized waistline	.54		

that preceded the crest with the yellow/orange, demonstrated a strong affinity with the green/blue cluster. Which cluster is currently forming as an intermediary type after the dominance of black is not yet very clear.

For the sake of completeness, we give here the four types, with the correlation between the curve of each characteristic and the curve of all other characteristics of the cluster.

The two fashion clusters that are most important for us are the yellow/orange cluster and, especially so, the black cluster, which we have taken as an indicator of the underlying insecurity and anxiety in society.

Our main concern here is the detection and quantification of the level of anxiety as the black type expresses it, and the corollary of the yellow/orange type that forms its psychological counterpart.

It was interesting to see to what extent the factor analysis could improve the results of the corollary matrix. They did indeed confirm them. When applied, the second factor gave high positive values for the greater part of the characteristics of the black and brown clusters and high negative values for the greater part of the characteristics of the yellow/orange and blue/green clusters.

Eliminating the weaker corollaries and the characteristics that were too strongly related with respect to content, we were able to reduce the number substantially. For the black type only five characteristics remained, for the yellow/orange only four.

Table 5.2:

black type	**orange-yellow type**
black	yellow, red and orange
dresses with low neckline	dresses with high neckline
skirt length: calf and maxi	skirt length: mini
non patterned dresses	patterned dresses
dresses with stripes	

The following graphs show precisely the evolution over time of each of both characteristics. It is not insignificant to note that for each of both types, colours as well as characteristic shapes and motifs are included.

Graph 5.1: Evolution of the yellow/orange type or the long wave of "happiness", 1956-2000

Sources: Libelle, Het Rijk der Vrouw, Flair, personal calculations

Graph 5.2: Evolution of the black type or the long wave of anxiety, 1956-2000

Sources: Libelle, Het Rijk der Vrouw, Flair, personal calculations

Table 5.3: Standard scores of the long wave of anxiety.

1956	-,08	1971	-,91	1986	,29
1957	,09	1972	-,87	1987	,35
1958	-,39	1973	-,74	1988	,43
1959	-,30	1974	-,07	1989	,33
1960	-,48	1975	,17	1990	1,08
1961	-,51	1976	,20	1991	,78
1962	-,62	1977	,31	1992	,51
1963	-,55	1978	,02	1993	,86
1964	-,84	1979	,42	1994	,74
1965	-,53	1980	,10	1995	,44
1966	-,80	1981	-,25	1996	,30
1967	-,65	1982	,10	1997	,27
1968	-1,06	1983	,35	1998	,81
1969	-1,08	1984	1,06	1999	,32
1970	-,97	1985	1,32	2000	,06

The result of this extensive statistical consideration and reduction is simply amazing. With the help of just five fashion characteristics, we have found a reliable indicator of the evolution of underlying anxiety in Western society. At this stage of our research, this is a daring hypothesis. Overall, there are yet more daring hypotheses. Indeed, our research is founded on a catalogue of dresses in Dutch-language weeklies. To what extent are these results valid for the Dutch-speaking regions? To what extent can they also indicate the underlying anxiety and insecurity in French, German, or English-speaking countries, or even in the United States of America?

There are no studies that can inform us about this and would allow us to say that the difference between the mass media in different countries lies only in the language and that the subjective contents would be the same. Of course, this assumption is not wholly improbable since we see that many countries can enjoy seeing the same motion picture on condition that it is dubbed in the national language.

Obviously, the ultimate test of the hypotheses we have set up until now is the test of practical experience. It implies that we ask ourselves, purely in an inductive way, which behaviour in our society can be interpreted as anxiety-driven behaviour or rather, which behaviour can be seen as functional with regard to the increase or decrease of underlying insecurity and anxiety or its opposite. It is not an easy choice, as we cannot use behaviour that fits the scope of defending one's immediate interest. Then there is a further — and twofold — problem. Even if we succeed in observing a number of phenomena of mass psychology in the second half of the 20th century, with their contemporary sources, and hence find corroboration of the correctness of our hypotheses, we are stuck with the problem of verifying our hypotheses with facts from the first half of the 20th century, the whole 19th century and the latter part of the 18th century. And what about the relation between a number of possible indicators and Kondratiev's price fluctuations?

We want to point out that all correlations [R] between the curves have been stated as Pearson correlations. Pearson correlations allow us to express the extent to which two sequences evolve in the same way over time but do not indicate a possible causal connection between both. In other words, as a consequence, the correlations we thus obtained are influenced by time. While examination of the graphs remains important, we did not give the level of significance of the correlations since the characteristics of the time sequences cannot be calculated correctly. In addition to this, we also calculated the partial correlations, which we checked as to the time effect. Apart from a possible time effect, these correlations indicate a direct connection with the long wave of anxiety — which we here considered as an independent variable — and the other variables we calculated.

5. First test: the long wave of anxiety in present-day society

Anxiety, marriage, and procreation

It seemed obvious that demographers could give us reliable statistics over the years. It is a commonly known fact that the decision to marry is interwoven with a common feeling of distrust and circumspection with regard to the future, as a result of which marriage is postponed or, conversely, the age at which people marry advances when they have a deep-rooted feeling of faith in the future. Births are of course closely related to this: how many children one will have, how early or how late one decides to have children...

Then again, the family is a field of demographic studies and serves as a practice field for statistics. The evolution of demographic data over a longer period in the past also confronts us with a number of non-recurrent data, demographic revolutions, which almost exclude a regular rising and falling of particular curves. There is the growth in the Fifties and then, in the Seventies, the use of contraceptives, because of which the number of unwanted pregnancies goes down and births will more closely reflect the parents' frame of mind and expectations for the future. Today, we are increasingly confronted with young people living together and thinking about whether or not to marry at a later stage. What effect will this have on the number of marriages and the age at which people marry?

Much has been written about the impact of demographic data on the economic evolution. The rise and fall of births for example can result in rising and falling numbers of consumers or in the work force.

Yet, demographers are well aware that their excellent numerical data cannot capture the drift of strictly defined causal connections. "It has been proven that it is strategic to study changes in families as reflectors of changes in society at large," W. Dumon writes. "There are so many factors involved in decisions on marriage and fertility (or other matters as well) that it is futile to reconstruct the whole process," Y. Ben-Porath sighs in an attempt to understand family behaviour from an economic point of view.

Table 5.4:

Births per 1,000 pop.	Correlation with the long wave of anxiety	
	Pearson correlation	Pearson correlation
Belgium, 1956 – 1998	-.69	-.05
Germany, 1956 – 1998	-.65	-.17
France, 1956 – 1998	-.79	-.44 **
Great Britain, 1956 – 1998	-.71	-.33 *
The Netherlands, 1956 – 1998	-.71	-.20
USA, (all inhabitants), 1956 – 1999	-.53	.06
USA, (whites), 1956 – 1998	-.42	.38 **
USA, (blacks), 1956 – 1998	-.51	.41 **

significance < .05, ** significance < .01, *** significance < .001

Source: see list of sources at the end of this chapter

Nevertheless, in spite of all these factors, the long wave of anxiety seems clearly visible to us in the following correlations and even more so when we visualize them in graphs.

The remarkable thing about births is the fact that their number decreases in the Sixties i.e. a number of years before the wave of anxiety reached its bottom or, on the other hand, before the wave of optimism reached its peak. This could indicate that we are dealing here with an even more sensitive indicator. The 1984 crest of the wave of anxiety corresponds quite precisely with the low of births in a number of countries, almost to the year. The ebb of the wave of anxiety beginning in the Nineties is again followed by an increase in the number of births, against all the expectations of quite a few demographers who ventured to make prognoses in the Eighties. Having a child is just not being approached with a "rational choice theory" by which the parents concerned would first weigh the economic situation and then, with regard to their conclusions, would decide to have a child or not. The fact that the correlation of births with the long wave of anxiety we expected manifests itself in partial correlations in two countries only is perhaps due to the fact that the recent rise is rather limited when compared to the sharp decrease as a consequence of the use of the pill since the Sixties.

A further indicator which can be said to reflect the way in which the present times are sensed are marriages and the age of the women at the time of birth of their first child. Since the 19th century, we know that in dismal times or when one fears dismal times ahead, marriage is postponed. Apart from this recurrent phenomenon, there is the fact that in the West — after the Swedish model — marriage is being postponed because of the increasing employment of women in the economic process. No matter how plausible these explanations may be, scores of studies on the subject seem to ignore the chronology. If this account is true, employment— as a result of it — should increase before the age at which one marries and has children increases. The widespread use of the pill has of course greatly reduced the number of enforced marriages and so increased the average age. Besides, we should bear in mind that living together instead of marrying also has its effect.

Table 5.5:

Marriages per 1,000 pop.	Correlation with the long wave of anxiety Pearson correlation	Partial correlation
Belgium, 1956 – 1999	-.66	-.13
Germany, 1956 – 1999	-.62	.09
France, 1956 – 1999	-.83	-.57 ***
Great Britain, 1956 – 1998	-.74	-.37 **
The Netherlands, 1956 – 1999	-.86	-.65 ***
USA, 1956 – 1998	-.12	-.27

* significance < .05, ** significance < .01, *** significance < .001

Source: see list of sources at the end of this chapter

Whereas most countries find that at the time when the long wave of anxiety rises, the number of marriages decreases, with exceptionally high negative correlations even in France, in Great Britain and in the Netherlands, Belgium and the Netherlands make an exception to the rule as if marriages had nothing to do with underlying anxiety. We surely need to study marriage behaviour in the United States. We have no explanation for this behaviour other than a simple ad hoc explanation.

As for the age at the time of marriage, we may expect that the decrease of anxiety since the Nineties will be followed by a decrease of the age: since anxiety decreases, there is no reason to postpone marriage. However, we see that even today marriage is postponed, for quite different reasons though. Increased emancipation led women to pursue a professional career. Besides, liberalised norms in the matter of marriage and living together allows ever more people to live together instead of marrying. For all these reasons the age at the time of a first marriage will no longer reflect anxiety-driven behaviour in spite of the fact that, isolated from the said factors, it would be an excellent indicator of increasing and decreasing anxiety.

On the other hand, we can use the age of the woman at the time of birth of her first child. To rule out the effect of living together, however, it is important that we consider births in and out of wedlock. You will find the correlations between the long wave of anxiety and the age of the woman at the time of birth of her first child in the following table 5.6. It gives data for Great Britain, the Netherlands and the United States as only these countries provide data concerning all first births, both in and out of wedlock.

Table 5.6:

Age at time of birth first child (in and out of wedlock)	Correlation with the long wave of anxiety Pearson correlation	Partial correlation
Great Britain, 1970 – 1995	.60	-.76 **
The Netherlands, 1956 – 1998	.75	.42 **
USA, 1960 – 1995	.86	.45 **

* significance < .05, ** significance < .01, *** significance < .001

Source: see list of sources at the end of this chapter

For two of the three countries, namely the Netherlands and the United States, a significant connection seems to exist between the age at the birth of a first child and the long wave of anxiety.

The labour market

In society, unemployment and available jobs are data that cannot directly be interpreted as behaviour resulting from the underlying anxiety of the people concerned. In spite of this they may be considered as side effects of a society that is dominated by anxiety.

Table 5.7:

Unemployment per 1,000 pop.	Correlation with the long wave of anxiety Pearson correlation	Partial correlation
Belgium, 1956 – 1999	.80	.52 ***
Germany, 1956 – 1999	.80	.51 ***
France, 1956 – 1999	.81	.58 ***
Great Britain, 1956 – 1999	.75	.42 **
The Netherlands, 1956 – 1999	.72	.45 **
USA, 1956 – 1999	.42	.37 **

* significance < .05, ** significance < .01, *** significance < .001

Source: see list of sources at the end of this chapter

If we examine the long curve of anxiety over a period of almost half a century and compare it with the curve of unemployment over the same period, we see that they are almost identical. This is somehow perplexing as it is obvious, as we already said, that unemployment could not be the direct consequence of a decrease or increase of the average level of anxiety in society. It is indeed not the unemployed who decide whether to become unemployed or to stay at work. This confronts us with a totally different fact, though it is of the highest possible importance for the aetiology of the long wave of anxiety. If we assume that anxiety in society naturally increases with increasing unemployment, increase or decrease in anxiety would have to follow the increase or decrease in unemployment. This is not the case. They move parallel with each other.

Graph 5.3: The long wave of anxiety and unemployment in Germany, 1956-2000

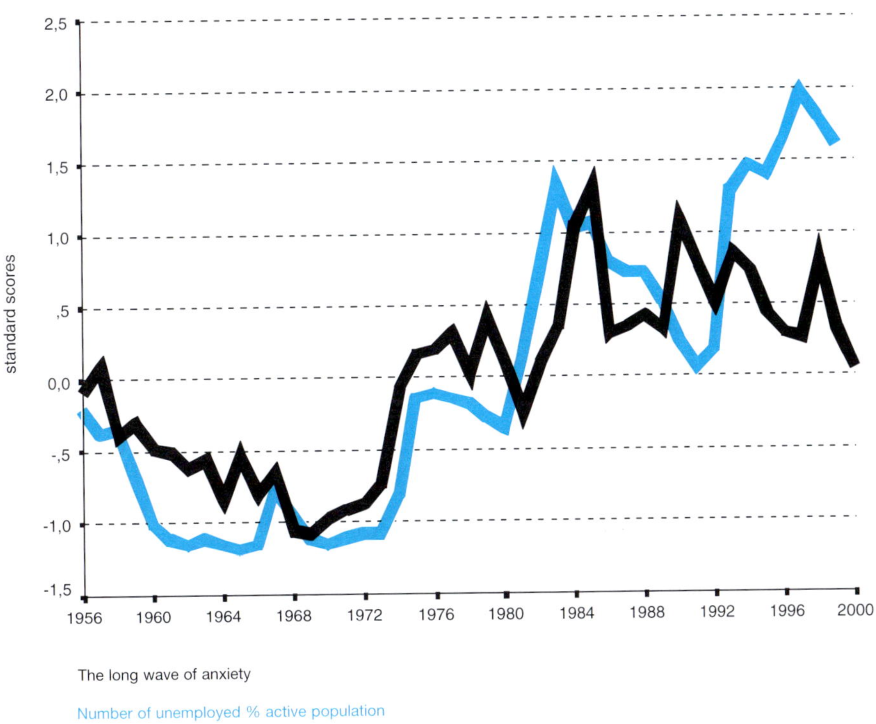

Source: A. Maddison (1991) and OECD

The economic fact of unemployment and everything that is connected with it cannot be the cause of anxiety. This does make it a little more difficult to see economic processes as fundamental causes of the long wave of anxiety and forces us in the direction of a rather autonomous development of the waves of anxiety and their opposite wave of optimism. The lack of a conclusive explanatory cause of the long wave of anxiety, be it in the economic or in the demographic sectors, or in other sectors of human behaviour, leads us to believe all the more that there is a sort of biorhythm in the cultural dynamics of social evolution. This could well be what J. Schumpeter has called "the animal spirits". It would also explain why, despite all the technological revolutions and economic scaling-up of the last two centuries, the rhythm of the long wave continues its beat. However, before we can verify such a hypothesis we need to do a lot more research. We shall confine ourselves to the description of the long wave of anxiety and functional anxiety-driven behaviour that results from it. The question of the cause of the long wave has not found a conclusive answer while it still was — due to Kondratiev — a problem of prices. How could we possibly explain the existence of a biorhythm of social evolution over time?

Additional specification of the above table concerning Belgium and the Netherlands follows. In fact, the table tells the same story: when anxiety is at a high point, the number of jobs is limited and vice versa. The remarkable part about this is that, here too, both curves fluctuate with such a remarkable correlation during forty-four years.

Table 5.8:

Total number of jobs	Correlation with the long wave of anxiety Pearson correlation	 Partial correlation
Belgium, among 15-64-year-olds, 1961 – 1998	-.80	-.40 **
The Netherlands, among 20-64-year-olds, 1957-1995	-.84	-.66 ***

* significance < .05, ** significance < .01, *** significance < .001

Source: see list of sources at the end of this chapter

Graph 5.4: The long wave of anxiety and jobs in the Netherlands, 1956-2000

Source: CBS

Investments

With investments, we find ourselves again in the field in which psychological factors may play an important role. Once they exceed the level of capital replacement, investments, in one way or another imply the expectation of a return. The question is on what those expectations are based. As soon as the general economic climate improves, the answer is simple: it is based on the expectation that the following year will be better than the last, and the reverse in a phase of recession. Except for the years of reversal, at the bottom or at the top of a long wave of the business cycle, maintaining this strategy can be totally wrong. Furthermore, we can include very many economic data in the decision whether or not to increase or cut back investment. Nevertheless, as shown in the table below, the wave of anxiety is not far away: increasing anxiety and decreasing investment appear to be closely linked by negative correlations. Germany, France, and the Netherlands above all, give evidence of high scores.

Table 5.9:

Investments in percentage of GNP	Correlation with the long wave of anxiety	
	Pearson correlation	Partial correlation
Belgium, 1960 – 1998	-.40	-.29
Germany, 1960 – 1998	-.68	-.41**
France, 1957 – 1998	-.56	-.40 **
Great Britain, 1957- 1998	-.11	-.19
The Netherlands, 1957 – 1998	-.84	-.62 ***

* significance < .05, ** significance < .01, *** significance < .001

Source: see list of sources at the end of this chapter

Further analysis of the Dutch data again shows how both curves are in fact attuned to each other. In 1969/70, after years of high-level activity, investments plunge downward until they stabilize in 1976/77. In 1980, the wave of anxiety gradually rises again until two years before it suddenly shoots up and begins to rise more sharply from 1982 onwards. In the same period, investments too take the plunge and reach rock bottom just before the wave of anxiety reaches its absolute low. The ebb of the wave of anxiety that follows it is, again, followed by a rise in investment, which now even slightly precede it. The fall in investment after 1990 however does not match the ebb of the wave of anxiety in the same period.

Suicides

If we ask the question of possible behaviour during a phase of increasing uncertainty and anxiety, suicide comes to mind as a potential functional behaviour. In that case, we suppose that a number of people with suicidal tendencies who stand on the threshold of proceeding to act will cross it and commit suicide under the pressure of increased or increasing existential anxiety whereas in a reverse phase of the long wave — a phase of increasing self-confidence and optimism — they would not have done so. Conversely, it seems obvious that the majority of suicides will not be influenced by the fluctuation of the long wave. To verify this we examined the correlation between the curve of suicides over a period of approximately forty years and the wave of anxiety. The result was surprising since the hypothesis appears to be valid for France, Belgium, the Netherlands and Great Britain. It is remarkable that in Great Britain the initially negative correlation of the long wave of anxiety with suicides becomes positive when we check for the effect of time, i.e., when we consider the long wave of anxiety as an independent variable.

Table 5.10:

Suicides per 1,000 pop.	Correlation with the long wave of anxiety Pearson correlation	Partial correlation
Belgium, 1956 – 1994	.74	.37 *
Germany, 1956 – 1997	-.28	-.05
France, 1956 – 1996	.82	.54 ***
Great Britain, 1956 – 1998	-.49	.44 **
The Netherlands, 1956 – 1998	.69	.30 *
USA, 1956 – 1997	.55	.10

* significance < .05, ** significance < .01, *** significance < .001

Source: see list of sources at the end of this chapter

If we look more closely at the situation in France, which has the highest correlation, we are surprised to see the macabre parallelism between the two curves, which again confirms the significance of the wave of anxiety and so the significance of the fashion trends. These trends are disclosed every year in August and by then give a clear indication for a great the majority of countries — though not for all — of the number of suicides that will be counted after 31 December of the same year.

Graph 5.5: The long wave of anxiety and suicides in France, 1956-2000

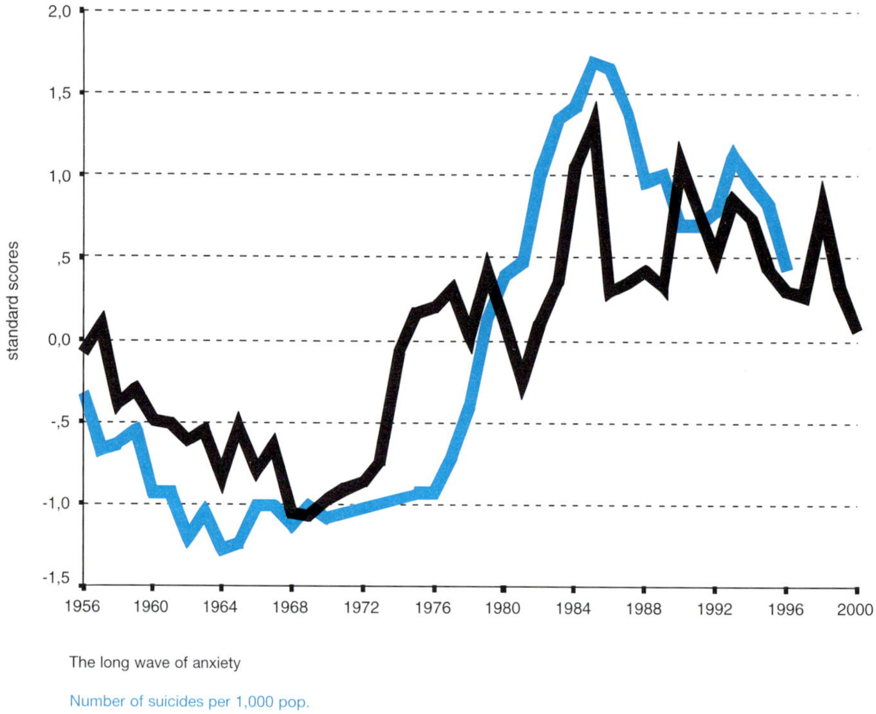

Source: Demographic Yearbook and INSEE

6. Second test: The relation between the long wave of anxiety and Kondratiev's series

The fact that the mass media did not use colour printing until the end of WWII prevents us from extending the method indicated above to the past, which on the face of it excludes a comparison with Kondratiev's curves. So, at first sight, the question of and the extent to which wholesale processes were a useful or worthless indicator of underlying anxiety appeared to be impossible to answer. On the other hand, it is a fact that historians currently use Kondratiev's curves to order and classify economic development during the 19th century. Fluctuations obviously have an impact on the state of mind in society, and, to the extent that falling prices reflect a downward economic trend, and vice versa, we can assume that Kondratiev's series of falling prices reflect increasing insecurity and vice versa. However, whether all this was limited to economic and materialistic insecurity — not to mention the problems it entails for the common people — or that there was a growing existential anxiety, which showed itself in a wide range of behaviour, could not be established on the basis of price fluctuations. In the aetiology of the long waves, this also makes it impossible to establish whether they are an endogenous phenomenon or if the direct or indirect source should be sought outside the economic world.

The situation changed when we were able to examine an American study of fashion, which is in every way remarkable. As long ago as 1919, A.L. Kroeber published an extensive series of characteristics of women's fashion in the *American Anthropologist.* As some academic authorities considered working with long-term series as Marxist, the author and his co-author J. Richardson did not publish their *Three Centuries in Women's Dress Fashions: A Quantitative Analysis* until 1940. They also included all numerical data. *Three Centuries* deals only with tailoring characteristics, not with colours or textile designs, which are an essential part of the construction of the wave of anxiety as sketched above. Then again, those data were promising since we have seen to what extent tailoring characteristics together with colour and motifs form an integral part of the whole. Nevertheless, was this *pars pro toto* not insufficient? There was no room either for critical doubt about the representativeness of the dresses since for a certain number of years the authors had no more to show than a single dress in a painting. Apart from that, the authors did not count summer dresses, which are quite recent, but "women's evening and formal dresses", which had a less fleeting existence. Finally, the authors mainly examined the winter months, and every now and then springtime when no material for the preceding year could be found.

A quick answer could be found as to these possible points of criticism by calculating the correlations between each of those characteristics and the series of figures given by Kondratiev. Both series run from the end of the 18th century until the beginning of the period between the two wars of the 20th century. The results were remarkable. The authors may have developed a complicated method for measuring their fashion characteristics, such as the distance from the mouth to the bottom of the centre front of the skirt. Below we convert it into more understandable language.

If we look at the correlations of the six time series and Kondratiev's — which are the wholesale prices in Great Britain, France, and the United States, based on annual figures — we get the following remarkable table.

Table 5.11:

Traits or features of dresses Richardson and Kroeber 1788 - 1934	Correlation with Kondratiev's cycle England 1780-1922		U.S.A. 1791-1922		France 1858-1922	
	Pearson correlation	Partial correlation	Pearson correlation	Partial correlation	Pearson correlation	Partial correlation
1. Length of skirt or dress	-.55	-.62***	-.53	-.59***	-.69	-.72***
2. Length of waist or height of the waistline	-.65	-.57***	-.69	-.61***	-.37	-.53***
3. Length or depth of décolletage	.10 -	.13	-.17	.02	.08	-.005
4. Width of skirt at its hem or base	-.33	-.32***	-.40	-.40***	-.12	.14
5. Width or thickness of waist	.59	.56***	.68	.67***	.48	.52***
6. Width of décolletage across the shoulders	-.17	-.24**	-.24	-.39***	-.11	.08

* significance < .05, ** significance < .01, *** significance < .001

It is amazing to find such a high correlation between wholesale prices and four or five fashion characteristics in almost one and a half century. For the length of the skirt and the height and prominence of the waist, partial correlations indicate a significant connection between all three countries, independent of the influence of time. The correlation of the width of the skirt and the width of the décolletage across the shoulders with the Kondratiev' cycle for Great Britain and the United States are also worth mentioning. It is also amazing to see the extent to which American fashion characteristics correlate with the British and with French wholesale prices. This clearly proves that even then the fashion business had an international dimension.

To get a clear view of the peaks and lows we show a few series.

According to the charts, one can see more or less clearly that Kondratiev's phases reach their peaks around 1811, 1871, and 1921. When reading the charts one should take into account that the Kroeber and Richardson's cycles span three centuries whereas Kondratiev's only one and a half.

Graph 5.6: Length of skirt or dress and the Kondratiev cycle for the USA, 1791-1936

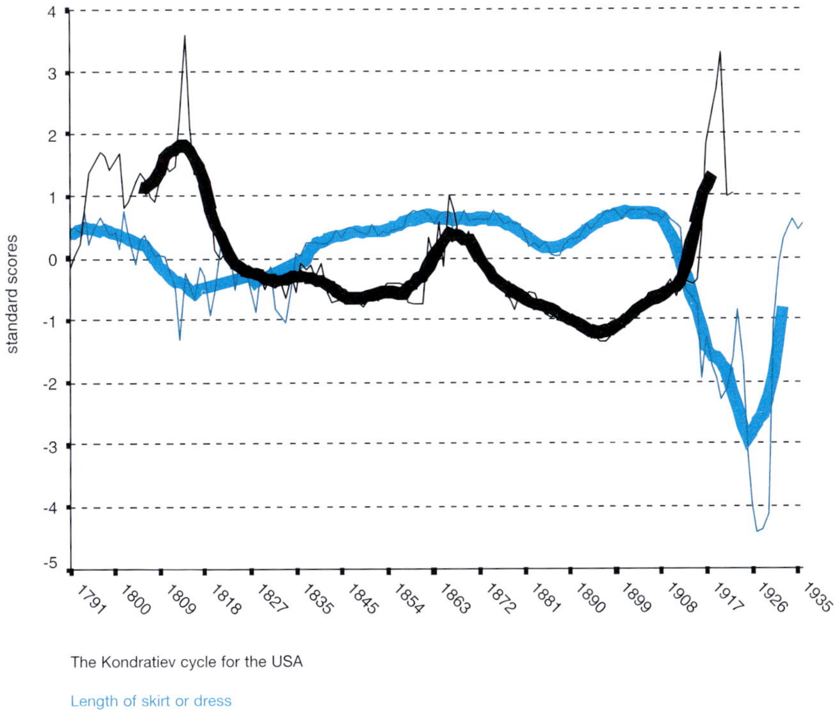

Per annum and 9-year moving averages
Source: J.Richardson and A.L. Kroeber (1940); N. Kondratiev (1926)

Oddly enough, the critical questions we put before appear not to be of the kind that disturb or obscure the long-wave character of a century and a half of fashion characteristics, or even make them invisible. Some of the curves are almost replicas of Kondratiev's cycle. Four out of six characteristics concern length, waistline, and width. In the previous chapter, we had also, directly or indirectly, included these tailoring characteristics in the curve of anxiety, which we have deduced from the 20th century material, even though in the end they do not appear strongly in the reduced model that we constructed. There is still another lesson we can draw from these correlations and which in fact has a bearing on the fashion phenomenon itself. The organic connection the clusters show is of the kind that even if a certain number of characteristics are absent, the remaining characteristics follow the same trend due to the high correlations. In other words, in the

Graph 5.7: Length of waist and the Kondratiev cycle for England, 1780-1936

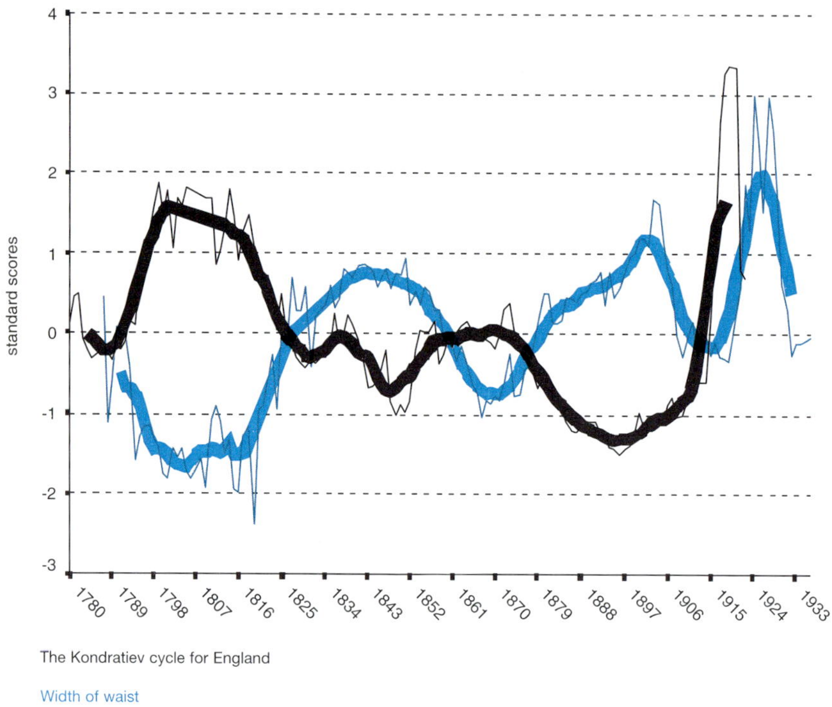

Per annum and 9-year moving averages
Source: J.Richardson and A.L. Kroeber (1940); N. Kondratiev (1926)

fashion trend situation, the *pars pro toto* is possible. A characteristic that is completely out of tune is the length or depth of the décolletage. Here, however, we must ask ourselves what a décolleté meant in the middle of the 19th century. It is probable that a certain form of low neck was a constant element of "women's evening or formal dresses." We do not have a definitive answer to that question.

We may conclude that Kroeber and Richardson's fashion characteristics can be seen as the wave of anxiety from the late 18th century until the beginning of the 20th century.

Ultimately, these data also enable us to ask the question of the synchronism or asynchrony of the two curves in view of the question we have asked

Graph 5.8: Width or thickness of the waist and the Kondratiev cycle for the USA, 1791-1936

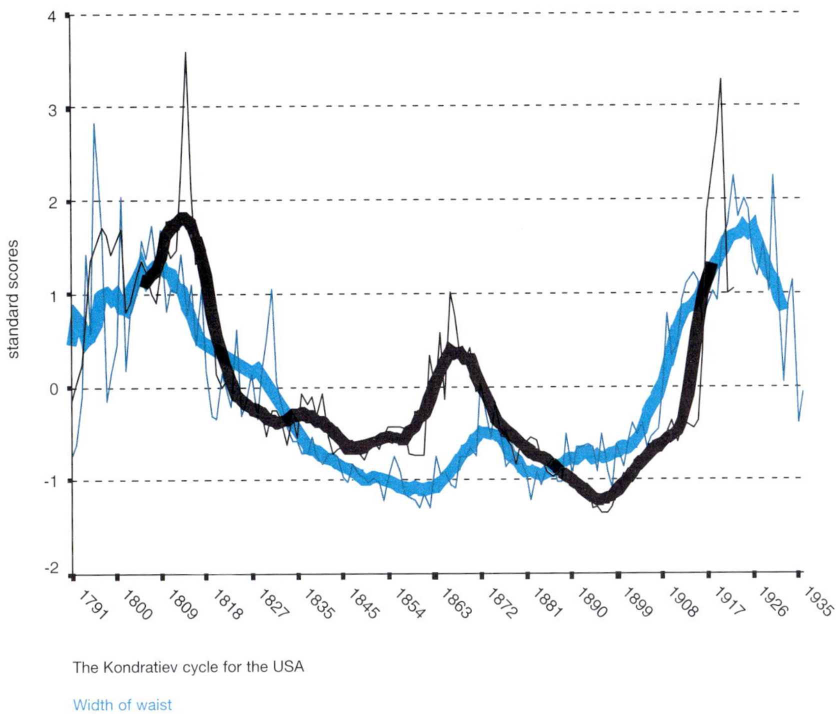

Per annum and 9-year moving averages
Source: J.Richardson and A.L. Kroeber (1940); N. Kondratiev (1926)

before: does the fluctuation of prices cause the variation of fashion and hence the wave of anxiety, or the reverse. In other words, what is the quickness of response of prices to the wave of anxiety or the quickness of response of the wave of anxiety to prices?

Important indicators here are that the length of the dress, the height or the emphasis on the waistline, and the width of the dress run synchronously — either positively or negatively — with wholesale prices. All in all, we cannot determine whether Kondratiev's cycle or the fashion cycle comes first or follows the other. Hence, the economic situation cannot be the cause of increasing or decreasing anxiety as it would chronologically precede the wave of anxiety, whereas increasing or decreasing anxiety results in an immediate change of behaviour and no chronological precedence is required in order to allow it to be the cause of change in the economic situation.

This projection into the past also has a practical consequence: from now on we can without hesitation use Kondratiev's cycle from the end of the 18th until the middle of the 20th century as a perfect reflection of the wave of anxiety. This also means that very many events from that time period, which have until now essentially been considered as linear consequences of economic trends, rest on too narrow a basis and have in fact to be considered as consequences of the wave of anxiety. Strict economic determinism is no longer tenable. It is a determinism of a different kind, of which we do not yet know very much, that in a certain way governs the economic processes and in another the cultural dynamics of society. At last, we have been able to identify Schumpeter's "animal spirits."

It is obvious that these hypotheses suggest a sort of biorhythm of social evolution and that we will still need to do more research to determine its actual range. Nevertheless, our hypotheses allow us to foresee the future and may perhaps have their own implications as to outlining marketing policies.

7. List of sources

Table 5.4: **Births per 1,000 pop.**
Belgium: 1956-1988:International Historical Statistics (Europe);1989-1995: Demographic Yearbook; 1996-1998: Council of Europe
West Germany: 1956-1988: International Historical Statistics (Europe); 1989-1998:Council of Europe
France: 1956-1988: International Historical Statistics (Europe); 1989-1995: Demographic Yearbook; 1996-1998: Council of Europe
Great Britain: 1956-1988: International Historical Statistics (Europe); 1988-1994: Demographic Yearbook; 1995-1997: Council of Europe
The Netherlands: 1956-1988: International Historical Statistics (Europe); 1989-1995: Centraal Bureau voor Statistiek (CBS); 1996-1998: Council of Europe
USA: total population: 1956-1999: National Center for Health Statistics; *whites:* 1956-1959: International Historical Statistics (The Americas); 1960-1998: National Center for Health Statistics; Remark: up to 1980 race of the child, since 1981 race of the mother; *blacks:* 1956-1963: International Historical Statistics (The Americas); 1964-1998: National Center for

Health Statistics; Remark: up to 1980 race of the child, since 1981 race of the mother

Table 5.5: Marriages per 1,000 pop.
Belgium: 1956-1988: International Historical Statistics (Europe); 1989-1999: Eurostat: Yearbook '97, Yearbook 2000, Statistics in Focus, 10/2000, Theme 3.
Germany: 1956-1985: International Historical Statistics (Europe); 1985-1988: the mean value of International Historical Statistics (Europe) and Eurostat; 1989-1999: Eurostat: Yearbook '97, Yearbook 2000
France: 1956-1988: International Historical Statistics (Europe); 1989-1999: Eurostat: Yearbook '97, Yearbook 2000
Great Britain: (England and Wales) : 1956-1988: International Historical Statistics (Europe); 1989-1998: Eurostat: Yearbook '97, Yearbook 2000
The Netherlands: 1956-1988: International Historical Statistics (Europe); 1989-1999: Eurostat: Yearbook '97 en Yearbook 2000
USA: 1956-1988: International Historical Statistics (The Americas); 1989-1995: Eurostat: Yearbook '97; 1996-1998: National Center for Health Statistics. Births, Marriages, Divorces and Deaths. Provisional Data for 1998

Table 5.6: Age at time of birth first child
Great Britain: 1970-1995: Council of Europe
The Netherlands: 1956-1998: Centraal Bureau voor Statistiek (CBS)
USA: 1956-1995: National Center for Health Statistics

Table 5.7: Unemployement per 1,000 pop.
Belgium: 1956-1989: Maddison, A., 1991, Dynamic Forces in Capitalist Development. A long run comparative view., 1991, Oxford University Press.; 1990-1999: O.E.C.D.: Standardized Unemployment Rates
Germany: 1956-1989: Maddison, A., 1991, Dynamic Forces in Capitalist Development. A long run comparative view. 1991, Oxford University Press.; 1990-1999:O.E.C.D.: Standardized Unemployment Rates
France: 1956-1997: O.E.C.D.: Labour Force Statistics; 1998-1999: O.E.C.D.: Standardized Unemployment Rates
Great Britain: 1956-1989: Maddison, A., 1991, Dynamic Forces in Capitalist Development. A long run comparative view., 1991, Oxford University Press.; 1990-1995: Eurostat; 1996-1999: O.E.C.D.: Standardized Unemployment Rates
The Netherlands: 1956-1989: Maddison, A., 1991, Dynamic Forces in

Capitalist Development. A long run comparative view., 1991, Oxford University Press.; 1990-1999: O.E.C.D.: Standardized Unemployment Rates

USA: 1956-1988: International Historical Statistics (The Americas); 1989-1995: Eurostat; 1996-1999: O.E.C.D.: Standardized Unemployment Rates

Table 5.8: Total number of jobs

Belgium: 1961-1998: Ministerie van Arbeid en Tewerkstelling

The Netherlands: 1956-1995: Centraal Bureau voor de Statistiek (CBS)

Table 5.9: Investments in percentage of GNP

Belgium: 1960-1998: Nationale Bank van België

Germany: 1960-1998: Statistisches Bundesamt Deutschland (SBD)

France: 1956-1998: Institut National de la Statistique et des Etudes Economiques (INSEE)

Great Britain: 1956-1998: Office for National Statistics (ONS)

The Netherlands: 1956-1998: Centraal Bureau voor de Statistiek (CBS)

USA: 1956-1998: Bureau of Economic Statistics (BEA)

Table 5.10: Suicides per 1,000 pop.

Belgium: 1956-1987: Demographic Yearbook; 1989-1994: Nationaal Instituut voor Statistiek (NIS)

West Germany: 1956-1990: Demographic Yearbook; 1990-1997: Statistisches Bundesambt Deutschland (SBD), Statistisches Jahrbuch

France : 1956-1990: Demographic Yearbook ; 1990-1996: Institut National de la Statistique et des Etudes Economiques (INSEE), Annuaire Statistique de la France

Great Britain (England and Wales): 1956-1991: Demographic Yearbook; 1986-1998: Central Statistical Office, Annual Abstracts of Statistics

The Netherlands: 1956-1992: Centraal Bureau voor Statistiek (CBS): 95 jaren statistiek in tijdreeksen; 1993-1998:Centraal Bureau voor Statistiek (CBS): Kwartaalbericht Rechtsbescherming & Veiligheid 96/4, Statistisch Jaarboek, 2000

USA: 1956-1989:Demographic Yearbook; 1989-1996: National Center for Health Statistics; 1997: US Census Bureau: Statistical Abstracts of the USA

6. Twenty functional anxiety-driven behaviours: today and tomorrow

Introduction

In the following chapter, we will attempt to illustrate — still in an evocative but now more systematic way — a number of concrete behavioural changes that we have seen in the twenty years from 1970 to 1990. We will try to indicate in what way they can be seen as functional anxiety-driven behaviour with regard to the descending Kondratiev wave or more correctly, the ascending wave of uncertainty and existential anxiety, i.e. the new wave of anxiety we have constructed. Given the probable certainty that after a descending phase — the years before and after 1990 — a period of decreasing uncertainty and existential anxiety, an upward economic trend will follow, we can — on the basis of the theory we have developed in the preceding chapters — make prognoses about the behaviour we may, with a high probability, expect to develop in the two coming decades. If the rhythm of rising and falling of the long wave in the coming decades is the same as in the past two centuries, we can expect the bottom of the anxiety curve, and thus the peak of the economic boom, around 2015-2020. These long-term prognoses allow us to distance ourselves completely from the traditional source of statements about specific future behaviour: intuition. To this day, almost everyone who studies future behaviour sees intuition as his only source of knowledge. We do not doubt its value when it comes to describing the subjective experience of one's own times. However, it is at the very least rather hazardous to make statements about the behaviour of people in a society that lies years ahead of us and cannot possibly be experienced subjectively — i.e. based on intuition alone — by our contemporaries.

We can only speak about changes of behaviour that are in some way or other related to the evolution of the new long wave and not about changes that are relatively independent of the rise and fall of the average level of angst in society. In the social process, many other forces are at work which unquestionably determine a number of behavioural changes in large sections of society. We cannot and will not discuss these here.

Formulating prognoses always involves risks, which every scientist wants to avoid: prognoses may prove to be wrong; the repercussions on his reputation could be fatal. Yet, he cannot avoid the confrontation with reality since it is the ultimate test of the veracity of his theory.

Actually, there is always some uncertainty about the definition of expected behaviour. The causal chain first confronts us with the subconscious evolution of the average level of angst in society. Within the existing cultural context, this common social anxiety seeks possible functional behaviour that can be accepted, imitated, and so on. It is possible that in different periods of culture, in the coming evolution too, other behaviour will be available to lessen the level of anxiety, behaviour that will perhaps prove to be more efficient than the current behaviour that fluctuates with the long wave. On the other hand, we must also assume that such changes will develop by gradual stages, as the evolution of the long wave in the past and the corresponding behaviour have demonstrated. At any rate, from the behavioural functionalist viewpoint new behavioural patterns can easily be detected.

Illustrations, proof, and retrognoses

We have illustrated and, wherever possible, diagrammatised the results of our research into behavioural changes in the masses. Some of these results we have mentioned in the text, with the necessary references.

The illustrations are mainly drawn from covers of mass media such as *Der Spiegel*, *Newsweek* and *Time*. The purpose of this is an attempt to evoke the spirit of the times, a means of identification for the older reader and, for the younger, a suggestion to help understand the frame of mind in which the behaviour we describe in the text was displayed in a past he is not really familiar with.

The graphs depict retrognoses that have been corroborated by research. What does that mean? It means that if the hypotheses that have been developed on the basis of the mass-psychological interpretation of the long waves from a behavioural functionalist view of the fluctuation of normal anxiety are correct, they must have existed, in a statistically significant way, in the past. In other words, they are prognoses projected into the past. The charts depict a comparison of the frequency of specific anxiety-driven behaviour with the curve of anxiety that was reconstructed in the previous chapter on the basis of fashion characteristics. One might question how many such comparisons we need to consider a theory to be "proven." In this case, there is no scientific answer in the sense of a definite figure. Every additional study will constitute an additional element.

1. Family

As we explained in the preceding chapter, when we described the dresses, we did not only register the colours but other characteristics such as length, sleeves, the décolleté, whether or not the waistline is accentuated, and so on. Statistically, a number of these characteristics form a cluster and more or less evolve together. Skirts are shortest, for example, at the peak of a long wave and become longest just before the declining phase. At the peak of the last ascending wave, yellow, orange, red and sometimes extremely short skirts have no décolletage either, or sleeves, and the waistline is not accentuated. In this period — a period of strongly progressive women's liberation — the typically feminine formal characteristics are not accentuated. Conversely, in the period 1970-1990, this is, to an increasing degree, the case. The closer we approach to the economic slump, the longer and darker the dresses become; the feminine silhouette — thus the women themselves — completely changes: fashion shows an increasing accentuation of typically feminine forms: a deeper décolletage and a more pronounced waistline and hips, among other things. Women revert to their "typical" sex stereotype, whereas many achievements of the last emancipation period are maintained. Has it anything to do with increasing anxiety? Apparently it does.

For the above conclusions drawn from changes in fashion to be probable, a possible return to the woman's traditional role pattern ought to be observable in other types of behaviour; otherwise, those changes should be regarded purely as one of the mysteries of fashion. If we then compare relevant types of behaviour with the course of the Kondratievs, it emerges that the peak of the long wave in the Seventies coincides with the prime of the progressive movement of women's emancipation in the West (illustrated for instance by the so-called unisex hairstyles: the same cut for men and women).

With the increase of uncertainty and anxiety in the last two decades, the whole emancipation movement has gradually declined (in the West). Conversely, the old traditional family, which in the flourishing period of the women's emancipation movement had been pushed to the background, regains importance. The conventional family even acquires anew the status of argument in the context of political struggle. In more general terms, this means that the peaks of the long waves, i.e. the insubstantial presence of basic anxiety, have a positive influence on the women's liberation movement, and vice versa. The return to traditional role patterns implies the restoration of the traditional family and all that that entails: the house, the interior and the children. Since insecure, anxious people experience the world as uncertain and anxiety-inducing, the family, the home becomes a safe haven in which one dares to abandon one's "normal", angst-ridden behaviour.

This new, changed psychological function of the family is also reflected in domestic architecture, with its clearest illustration in the architectural magazines: the nearer one comes to the present time, the smaller the windows (large windows are perceived as unsafe); they are increasingly provided with solid wooden shutters; the house may even be surrounded by an alarm installation. All this appears to indicate a concern for safety and protection, but in the last analysis, it functions to acquiesce the inner anxiety. This also explains why "cocooning" became so fashionable at the end of the eighties. It is characteristic for a period of increasing uncertainty and anxiety.

Within the increasingly cosy living environment, the father once again becomes the rather authoritarian father, anew complemented with the typical motherly mother — for the return to the older role patterns applies not only to the woman but also to the man. The insecure and anxious father would perhaps have felt threatened by a strong, emancipated woman; with the rather submissive wife, the motherly mother, he feels completely at ease. The woman thus unconsciously adapts to the situation, as she herself feels increasingly safe with a "strong", more authoritarian, traditional father, familiar from previous low points; the man equally responds to her requirement. One of the elements of this role-play, which makes this evolution externally visible, is precisely women's fashion, and in particular, an increasing emphasis of the typical female shape as described above. At the peak of the long wave, on the other hand, the prime moment of the miniskirt, of the colours yellow, orange and red, nothing is accentuated, and "typical" male and female roles are muted as much as is possible.

In more general terms, the grave uncertainty of the descending wave has the effect of loading the family with an additional function within the mechanism of anxiety reduction. Because the partner plays an essential role in the process of mutual attenuation of anxiety, he or she also becomes much more important than is the case during a period of low basic anxiety. This implies that much stronger claims are made on the partner, for instance with regard to marital faithfulness. Hence, marriage as an institution becomes much more important; however, if the high expectations are not fulfilled, the decision to divorce will be made much faster. In this perspective, the increased divorce rate can be seen as the consequence of the higher rigidity of marriage morals, which are partly subjected to the reduction of anxiety.

Graph 6.1: The long wave of anxiety and the mean age of the woman at birth of her first child, in Germany, 1956 - 2000

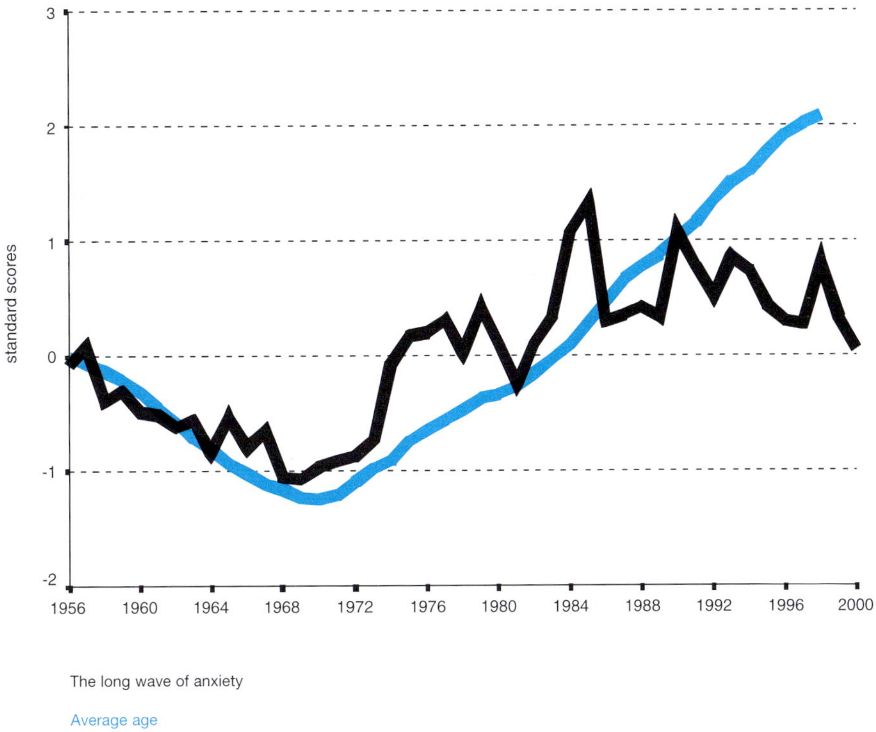

Source: Council of Europe

Graph 6.2: The long wave of anxiety and the marriages in the Netherlands, 1956 – 2000

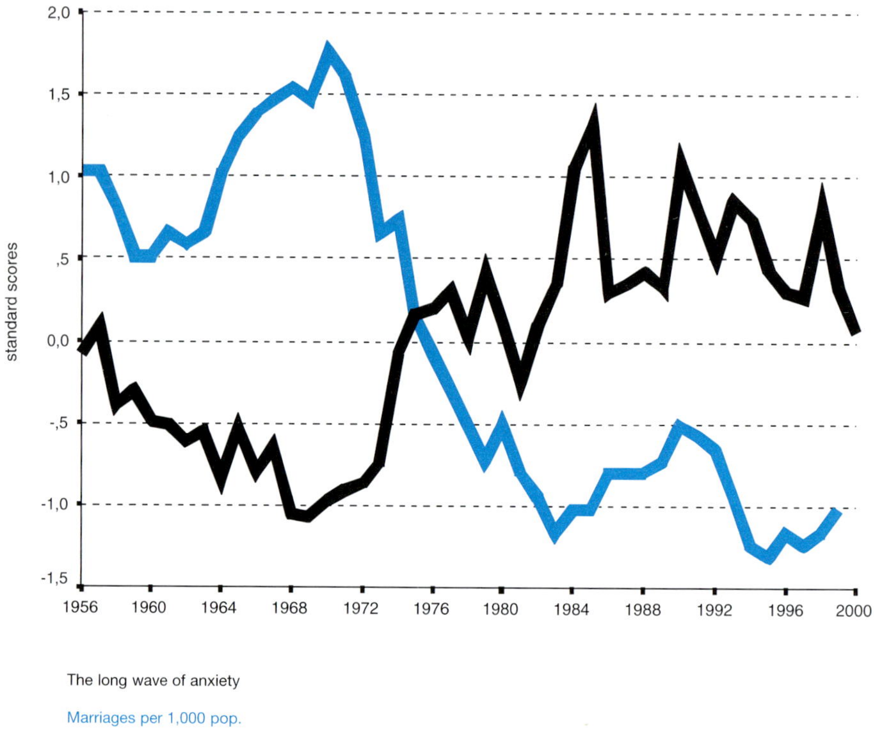

Source: European Historical Statistics and Eurostat

Obviously and completely logically in order to reduce anxiety, the child is given a much more important role in this newly traditional family. It becomes the nucleus that keeps the partners together, a component within the "strategies" developed to ward off the anxiety over the possible loss of the partner. Interaction with, and education of the child become important issues of pedagogical responsibility; children need to be schooled and disciplined, for otherwise they will not make it in the big bad world; for the child, no expense is too great.

All this stands in sharp contrast with the attitude towards the child adopted at the peak of the long wave: then, the conviction prevails that strict fathers and too many regulations and admonitions are harmful for the preservation of the child's innocence and the development of its self-confidence. More positively, one has great faith and confidence in, even respect for, the inherent potential of the child. The experiments of the British Summerhill School and especially the great distribution and popularisation of these ideas were typical of this outlook. A negative aspect of the emphasis on the independence of the child, seen from the current over-anxious perspective, was its inherent negligence. The children could do their own thing, there would always be someone looking after them — or so it was hoped.

Research into the quantitative evolution of the age of marriage and the number of children clearly shows that the increase and decrease of uncertainty has an effect on the number of children one will have and the age of marriage.

It is clear that also sexuality in general (see also section 7) comes to be involved in these alterations. The changes in fashion are a sufficient indication in themselves. On the other hand this material is so complex that only a few comments can be proffered at this point.

In his study on the mass psychology of Fascism, Wilhelm Reich, whom Freud called his best pupil, formulated an interesting thesis on the relation between the need for authority and an uninhibited, healthy experience of sexuality. Reich maintains that authoritarian attitudes, the need and admiration for authority, etc. diminish an uninhibited, healthy experience of sexuality, to the point of rendering it impossible; and conversely, that a healthy, uninhibited sexual life limits, if not precludes, the receptivity to authority.

If Wilhelm Reich's thesis is correct, it can be argued that the degree of difficulty in experiencing uninhibited, free and healthy sexuality, stands in direct relation with the extent to which the internalisation of authority and domination increases (which, as we saw, occurs during periods of increasing uncertainty, spontaneously in a family context with the restoration of the traditional family and re-emergence of the strong father; but which also finds expression in the political domain, for instance, as we shall see below). In descending phases of the conjuncture, sexuality becomes less direct, but searches for satisfaction via diversions, and thus with much less success. Perhaps this is an explanation of the vast market for sexual perversities today. It is, however, impossible to determine the expansion or contraction of this market with relation to the rhythm of the long waves. To arrive at firmer conclusions, it is imperative to conduct critical quantitative longitudinal studies on this and related matters. The next section, meanwhile, investigates the degree to which increasing uncertainty and anxiety during a descending wave alters the attitude to authority and domination in society.

2. The search for, the demand and creation of authority

The short-term process by which uncertainty and anxiety activates the attribution of authority is generally well known. In periods of chaos, revolution, or disasters, we often see the sudden emergence of individuals who are very rapidly considered to be leaders and who are obeyed without contestation. Here, this process is considered in a long-term perspective. That is to say, it is argued that the extent to which authority attribution (increasingly) occurs in the descending or low periods of the long wave, is a confirmation of the growing presence of underlying uncertainty and basic anxiety in society. The search for authority is not necessarily limited to the search for leading figures; it can also be a quest for leading principles, fundamental truths, and strict unabiding norms — to which we shall return in section 12.

We have already referred to the growing need for authority in the family, where the father is restored in his earlier role of person in authority. But if the hypothesis is correct, this must find expression in many other areas of human behaviour: in ordinary personal contacts, in business, in science, politics, religion, etc. It is important in this context to realise that this

Illustration 6.1: 1993, 28

search for authority and domination also creates authority and domination. In a situation in which no one needs authority, authority cannot establish itself, unless by force.

In politics this need for authority is abundantly present in the lowest points of the last two long waves, namely at the beginning of the 1930s and again round 1990. In both periods we saw a strong revival of extreme right-wing parties. Between the wars Hitler did not, by himself, achieve dictatorship; to that end he needed, and employed, the support and the votes of millions of Germans who were looking for someone like him, someone who proclaimed that only he could solve all problems, if only he was given absolute power. It is precisely this Führer-principle, this giving up of one's own responsibility, that is typical for extreme right-wing parties. The same applies to Fascist Italy and the Fascist parties that emerged at the time in virtually all European states. To establish that all those parties gained more influence is simply to establish that there were a continually growing number of people in that phase of the long wave who wanted to subject themselves uncritically to that command, to that political authority.

If the hypothesis of the long waves of basic anxiety is correct, it would have been predictable well in advance that extreme right-wing parties would again gain in popularity during the eighties — as was the case. It is equally probable that they will virtually have disappeared by the beginning of the next decade, precisely because of the pattern of the long wave, then ascending anew. To put it more strongly, such parties can never emerge in the peak phases of the long wave. Their success always disappears as the long wave rises again and self-confidence increases, or, as anxiety and uncertainty diminish. Phases of high basic anxiety are always dangerous for democracy. However, if they do not evolve into dictatorships, these parties disappear automatically. The argument presented here includes the full realisation of the extent to which it sheds a rather different light on traditional politicological and historical explanations.

The same mechanism is at work in the business world. During a phase of high basic anxiety, employees lack basic self-confidence. Consequently, they will present all their decisions to their hierarchical superiors for approval. But these superiors are themselves more anxious and insecure. As they no longer have confidence in themselves, they also have no confidence in their employees and thus increase their control on the latter. Gradually the firm will develop a hierarchic, pyramidal structure. Currently we find ourselves in the phase in which anxiety and uncertainty are fading away: employees are gaining self-confidence and have far less need for affirmation from above; the hierarchical superiors gain increasing self-confidence, and thus in their employees; it becomes possible to allow far more autonomous work, which also fits the employees better. It is thus not surprising that currently the market is flooded with volumes on business management which argue that lateral structures operate more efficiently than their pyramidal counterparts. But it is generally unacknowledged that it is the current abating of basic anxiety and uncertainty that underlies the causal relationship.

It is obvious that the concepts of obedience and discipline are intimately connected with authority, domination and hierarchy. In periods of great uncertainty and high basic anxiety, these concepts come to acquire the status of virtue. In education, for instance, they once more come to assume great importance, in contrast with the period of 1968-1972, when these were notions to be avoided. The argument then was that influence ought to be achieved through persuasive discussion leading to consensus, without recourse to "inhumane" means of force, such as obedience, discipline and correction.

3. Individualism

In this section, we examine the relation of increasing or decreasing individualism with increasing or decreasing basic anxiety. Many current publications state the problem unequivocally: they define our era as a period of explicit individualism. Some authors even speak of narcissism and thus misuse a typical Freudian concept. More generally, it is assumed that people are losing contact with their fellow human beings, which, in many cases, is attributed to television. Here this is argued to be an incorrect diagnosis, because it is based on the equation of two entirely different forms of individualism; I believe, moreover, that television-consumption is not the cause, but rather a consequence of the attitude under consideration.

For the attitude broadly commented on, and experienced as problematic, is not individualism in the common sense of the word, that is, the aspiration for independence by individuals who are self-sufficient because they are self-assured (a definition which generally implies a certain degree of egotism).

Individualism in a period of increasing anxiety can be defined as an attitude of ego-centricity (literally: being centred on the Ego), held by individuals who return to themselves, constitute a problem for themselves, want to know and scrutinise themselves, analyse themselves or want to be analysed by a third party, continue to stare at their own bellybuttons — whereas others and the world are demoted, respectively, to second and third place, that is, if there is any space left. This is a typical reflex of basic anxiety. As people become more anxious and insecure, they increasingly become a problem for themselves; they increasingly become self-preoccupied, and thus egocentric. This is comparable to some extent to someone in physical pain: their pain causes the attention of their consciousness to be oriented towards themselves. The changing relation to oneself also automatically affects the relation to others, or, the loss of self-confidence is automatically projected on to others: they are perceived as equally less certain and more anxious — which, in reality, is also the case. In short, a real weakening of the Ego takes place.

If it is the case, then, that in periods of a descending wave the level of basic anxiety in society increases, it must follow that a great number of people

Graph 6.3: The long wave of anxiety and investments in Germany, 1956 - 2000

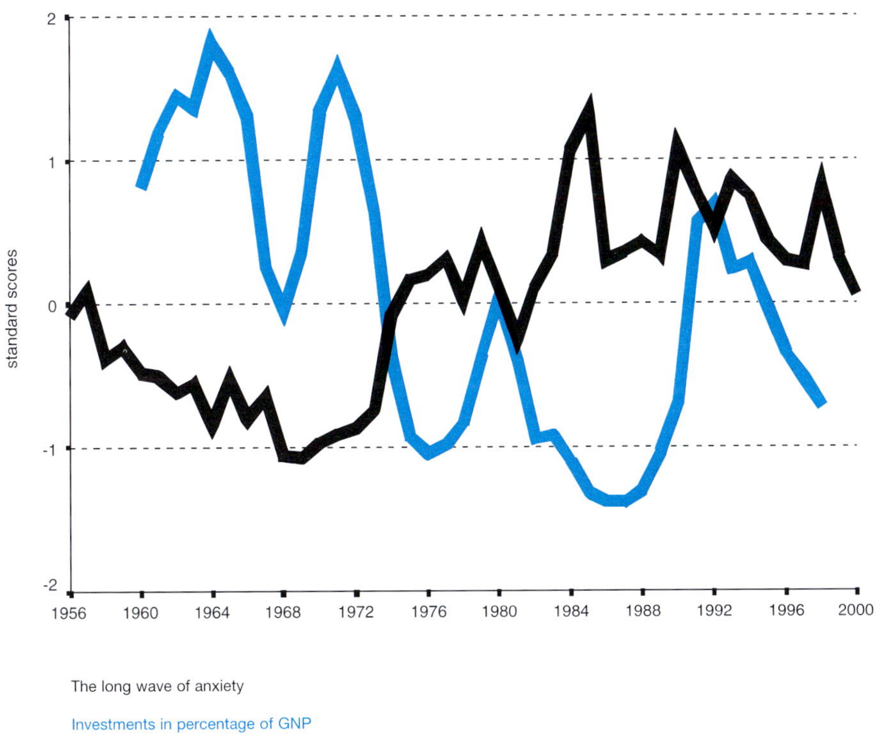

Source: Statistisches Bundesamt Deutschland

become more egocentric in the sense defined above. On the other hand, if there is such a general societal phenomenon, it ought to be observable on many different levels.

Graph 6.4: The long wave of anxiety and investments in the Netherlands, 1956 - 2000

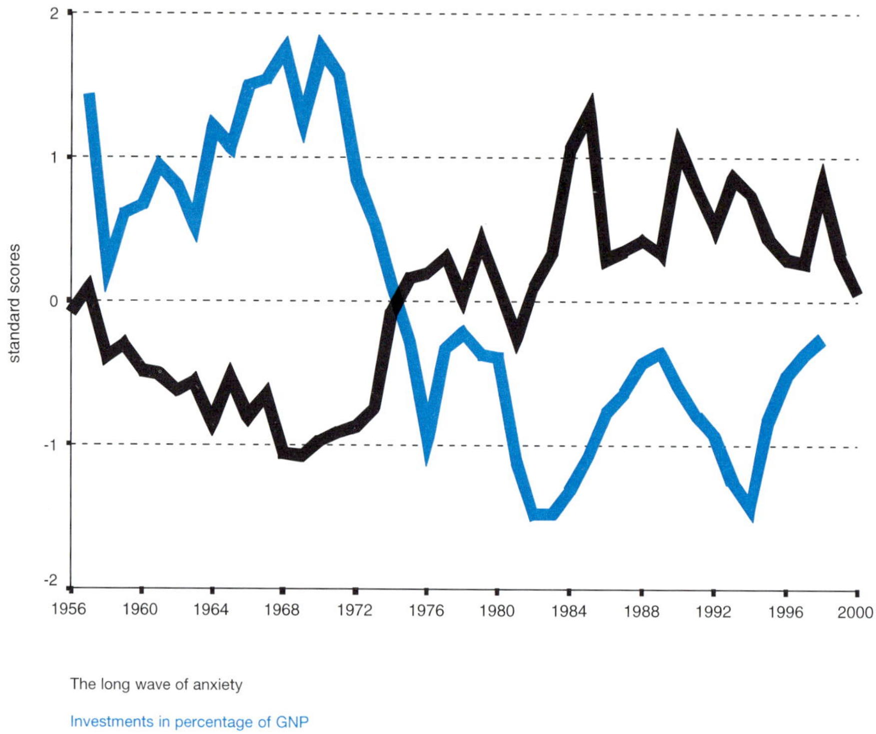

Source: CBS

One of the levels to be considered is the world of business. There, a lack of confidence in the future (which constitutes an intrinsic component of self-confidence) can be causally linked with less preparedness to invest as the low point of the wave approaches. Enjoyment of risks and anxiety rarely coincide. It could, however, be objected that investment is determined by many other factors.

A more persuasive case could, arguably, be made for the rising interest in ego-documents, such as diaries and memoirs. For these are genres

Graph 6.5: Number of published British diaries and Kondratiev's cycle for England, 1780 – 1942.

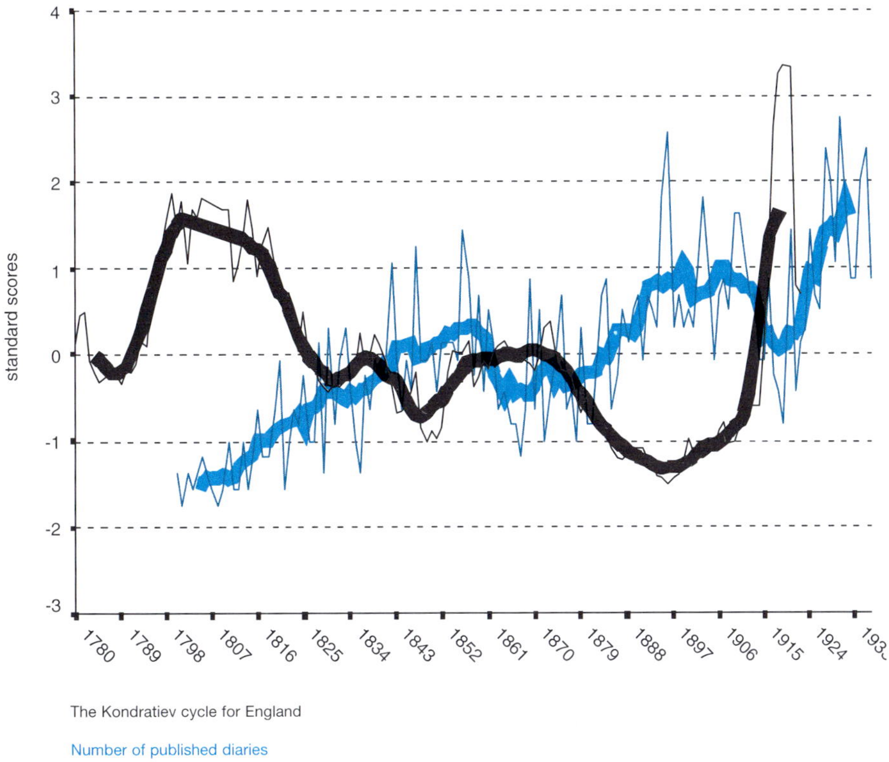

Per annum and 9-year moving averages
Source: W. Matthews (1950); N.D. Kondratiev (1926)

characterised by a high degree of interest in oneself (with the possible exception of travel diaries). Possible lines of inquiry are whether there is a correlation between the number of diaries entering on to the market and the evolution of the long wave; whether this was the case in the past and whether we could argue that today, in the nineties, the concern for the Ego is far greater than at the end of the Sixties or the beginning of the Seventies. Does this concern emerge for instance from the content of novels: is it indeed the case that literary personae are much more self-preoccupied (which is obviously always the case to some extent) now than at the end of the Sixties or the beginning of the Seventies? As the literary market is clearly also a market which delivers on demand, it may be hoped that these and related questions will inspire further research by reception sociologists in the literary sciences.[1]

Another area of possible investigation is the insurance behaviour of the average person. Is it the case, for instance, that many people, who at the peak of the long wave are oblivious to it, in a descending conjunctural wave become receptive to the advertisements of insurance companies and insure themselves against all sorts of accidents which might occur? At the peak of the long wave, basic anxiety is low; hence, although there is no less danger of possible accidents (arguably, the risk is even greater because one is more unaware and carefree), there is no need felt to insure oneself. Perhaps an attentive study of the insurance behaviour of the average citizen could shed light on this issue — evidently taking into account external factors which could equally determine this behaviour, such as the evolution of the living standard, the aging of the population, tax benefits, etc. We will return to this issue in section 8, where we discuss the mechanism of transforming anxiety into fear.

As suggested above, egocentrism is also influenced by an altered attitude to others. If one is insecure oneself, one does not expect much from the other (or conversely, too much, as is shown in the relation of extreme right-wing parties to their leader). For individuals who are growing more insecure, the contact with the other is time and again a problematic situation — which can be avoided by simply, safely, staying at home. And this is, arguably, the reason why a great number of people prefer to sit in front of their television rather than engaging in pastimes that involve others. Television and the flight into fiction in general (see below) will lose much of its attraction during the coming descending wave of anxiety, i.e. the ascending wave of conjuncture. In an economic upswing too, strong individualism is present but it is of a different kind. We see the origination and development a self-confident individual who wants to command respect and does not bow to authority, who attaches great value to quality of life and comforts which are more important to him than all kinds of expensive status symbols for instance. This individual is no longer a problem for himself. He looks at others, at the world, he is interested in infinitely diverse things and will usually be tolerant. It is the individualism of the citizen of a permissive society such as it existed in the descending wave of anxiety during the Sixties: in all conscience egotistical and materialistic, with a touch of

1 Described at length in: Helmut Gaus (2000).

playfulness, but always ready for a struggle if it implies a good deal of experiential value.

4. The degree of participation

The same mechanism which brings people to seclude themselves and, safely sheltered within the family (cocooning), to avoid contact with third parties, paradoxically also leads to two reflexes in the opposite direction, namely to an increasing interest in corporate life and to an increasing participation in mass manifestations.

This paradox, however, becomes less puzzling when considered within the explanatory framework of the long waves of basic anxiety. The first argument then runs that the more uncertain one becomes, the more one is inclined to become a member of societies which somehow give the impression that they are useful — psychologically rather than materially useful. For the more insecure one becomes, the more one realises that individual initiatives achieve very little. What then does one expect from others in these circumstances? Support? Help? Advice? The knowledge that one should not stand alone in times of need? Or is the motivation more basic: is it the case that the anxious person simply does not want to be alone? The answers to these and related questions could be provided by a systematic quantitative longitudinal study of the real participation of members in the activities of those societies that have a (manifest or latent) assistance character. The general logic of the hypothesis suggests that the number of members of societies will increase in the descending phases of the long wave. Conversely, that number will decline in the coming twenty years, because then the alternative type of individualism will emerge, the individualism of self-secure, independence-seeking people who approach the future full of self-confidence and who connect without problems with others.

The second reflex, different from but intimately related to the readiness to associate oneself with others and to participate in corporate social life, concerns the participation in mass manifestations. Of a different order and therefore not considered here, are those manifestations which are organised in order to press for a direct, material benefit for the participants (such as union demonstrations). Relevant examples in the present context are, for instance, anti-nuclear marches, manifestations for the preservation of the environment and demonstrations against the infiltration of dangerous plants. The development of mass participation in cultural events as rock concerts must equally be included.

Political literature has made it generally known that participation in mass manifestations has the effect of lowering the consciousness of those present. The feeling of union with others created through that participation also generates a feeling of power. This implies that, at the same time, the feeling of basic anxiety is reduced. It is therefore logical to assume that in the descending periods of the long wave, the masses are strongly inclined to participate in grand manifestations, precisely to be able to experience this effect of anxiety reduction and, more importantly perhaps, to experience a (temporary) feeling of power. This submergence in crowds also implies that a loss of individuality does not appear in the least troublesome to the participants during periods of increasing uncertainty. Conversely, however, in periods of a descending wave of anxiety, i.e. an ascending conjunctural wave, and especially at its lowest point, individuals consider this mass behaviour very much as a loss of personality and independence: this type of manifestation then appeals to far fewer people. This could (at least partially) explain why the anti-Vietnam demonstrations before the conjunctural long-wave peak of 1971 and those organised afterwards enjoyed such unequal success.

An additional element (on which more in section 13) is the internal approval of offensive expansionist aggression, even wars, during ascending periods of the long wave. This turns into aversion during its descending phase, characterised by increasing basic anxiety and uncertainty.

If the mechanism of the reduction of basic anxiety is responsible for growing mass participation, the latter will lose importance during the next two decades. For the past at any rate, the mechanism has clearly been demonstrated. Everyone is sufficiently acquainted with the political mass participation during the previous lowest point of the long wave, namely the 1930s. Mass participation was exploited to the full by a Hitler, a Mussolini — in fact, by the political leaders of all parties (sometimes the differences are not that great). They partially owed their successes to the manipulation of the participating masses, combined with their engagement with the need for leadership, domination and authority, as explained in section 2.

It has to be noted that, if the mechanism were indeed one of basic anxiety reduction, the same phenomenon should have occurred at the left of the political spectrum, where, obviously, the ideological definitions would have been totally different. However, comparative material that could confirm this supposition is not (yet) available.

5. Emotionality

The notion of "emotion" is one of the most central concepts in the analysis of the impact of increasing or decreasing anxiety on mass behaviour. In the literature, some go so far as to argue that anxiety is not accompanied by emotion, but rather that anxiety is emotion. Other authors write great volumes on emotions but, regrettably, never mention (basic) anxiety. There is nevertheless enough information which warrants the argument that the increase of insecurity and basic anxiety is paralleled by an equal increase in the emotionality of behaviour.

Since a descending conjuncture is characterised by the omnipresence of anxiety and uncertainty, the same period will be confronted with the omnipresence of intensified emotionality, which increasingly influences the perception of oneself, of others and of the world. Conversely, ascending phases of the long wave and in particular its peaks, that is, periods of growing certainty and self-confidence, will disclose mass behaviour which is far less dominated by emotionality.

A first methodological question arises as to how to define persons who react more emotionally, and how to distinguish them from less emotional, more rational, even more materialist individuals. The scope of the present paper does not permit the consideration, let alone the evaluation, of a great number of (theoretical) definitions. Both types of person, however, are commonplace, and it may be permissible to proceed with the implicit everyday meaning of the relevant terms.

A good illustration in point is the study by two German social scientists, subtitled *The Foundations of Collective Behaviour*.[2] In their analysis of the Bundesrepublik during the ascending period of the last long wave, the authors argue that a particular expression of emotionality, namely the capacity to mourn, declined (or, in their terms, even disappeared). It would follow that during the descending phases, and in particular at the lowest points, the readiness to mourn is very much present. Belgium offers at least two powerful examples: the death of two royals at the last two low points of the long wave, namely Queen Astrid in 1935 and King Baudouin in 1993;

2 Alexander and Margarethe Mitscherlich, *Die Unfähigkeit zu trauern. Grundlagen kollektiven Verhaltens*. Munich 1967.

and, in 1996, the White March in Brussels, the mass expression of sympathy and sadness over the murder of some young girls and of anger over the dismissal of the popular judge charged with the investigation. Meanwhile the capacity to mourn probably reached its highest point at the time of the death of Princess Diana in 1997.

Illustration 6.2: 1997, 39

Another methodological problem is the difficulty of "measuring" the rise and decline of the gradation of emotionality in society. It is clear, however, that such a yardstick is of extreme importance for the theory as a whole because of the close link between anxiety and emotionality: measuring the degree of emotionality almost equals measuring the degree of anxiety. In principle, all these types of behaviour would qualify for further research from which one can assume that they are somehow related to emotionality determined by basic anxiety. However, not all forms of behaviour are of determining importance. The question therefore turns to considering which types of mass behaviour are both sufficiently measurable and dependable to demonstrate the unequivocal increase of emotionality.

A first possibility could be a longitudinal study of advertisements and publicity. Since this form of communication, involving millions of dollars, is very sensitive to the impact of its message on the larger public, it reflects to a high degree the popular mood (and necessarily so, if it wants to remain efficient). According to the present hypothesis, publicity in general should have become more rational from the beginning of the 1990s onwards, since the public's anxiety will have started to diminish: increasingly, the more national, perhaps even technical, dimensions of the products should take centre stage. The notion of "quality" an important element in advertising, would then evolve from a romantic-emotional notion to a technical-rational concept.

Although possibly laughable at first, a second form of behaviour worth investigating is the increased ownership of pets, in particular of dogs, since the 1970s. For it must be obvious that the relationship with pets is in the first and probably even last analysis, a purely emotional matter. A continuous increase in pet ownership indicates indisputably that an increasing number of people need such a relationship. In countries with taxation on dogs, the quantitative growth is clearly visible since the Seventies. But an even clearer example is constituted by the growing consumption of medicines for dogs. From our contacts with the pharmaceutical industry, it has emerged that this type of medicine has been an important growth sector in the Seventies and eighties. However, for a few years, that is, at the end of the lowest point of the long wave, growth

Illustration 6.3: 1976, 5

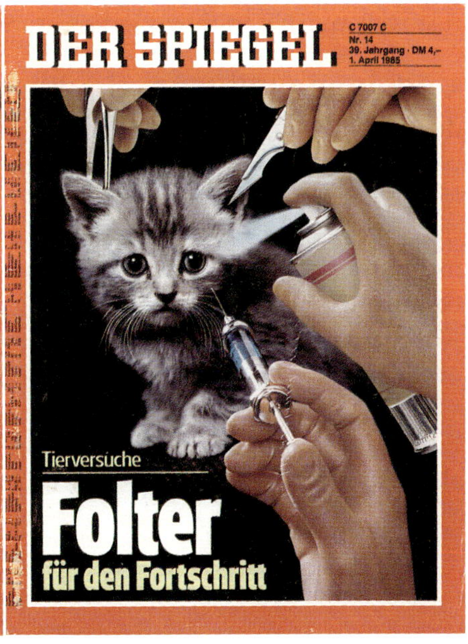

Illustration 6.4: 1985, 14

has stagnated. It remains to be explained, however, how that stagnation has been accompanied by a rising consumption of medicine for cats. In more general terms, it is important to establish to which degree the attitude towards pets constitutes an adequate parameter for the definition of growing emotional involvement and thus for increased emotionality in general. The findings of research on pets will need to be balanced with the study of the degree to which the growing percentage of elderly people (who, as is generally known, are in the habit of keeping pets), contributes to this growth.

A second instrument of measurement, on which serious academic research is already available, is the emotionalisation of language. The usefulness of this instrument can be illustrated by reminding oneself of the emotional quality, the pathos, of the language of the political leaders during the inter-war years. The language usage arguably constitutes one of the best instruments to define the position of the average level of basic anxiety in society. Of particular interest is the language of speakers and writers who address themselves to the masses and expect effective impact from their words, such as politicians, journalists, columnists and possibly even literary writers. So far, however, research has been limited to the analysis of political language usage. Since the latter has a great affinity with publicity, in that they are both employed with the purpose of direct effect, it can be assumed that politicians, and in particular successful politicians, adapt their language relatively quickly to the mood movements of their target audience.

Supported by linguistic research, C. De Landtsheer has focussed in her doctoral dissertation on the frequency of metaphors as one of the parameters of the degree of emotionality in language. Because of their long-term quality, she selected as primary sources for this research project the editions of newspapers. The global curve of the frequency of metaphors, which was thus reconstructed for the nineteenth and twentieth centuries, shows a strong negative correlation with the long wave of Kondratiev. De Landtsheer has hereby provided an important confirmation of the longitudinal and cyclical evolution of emotionality in society.[3]

Finally, it can be argued that the "romantic phases", especially in art history, also indicate heightened emotionality in ascending periods of the long wave

3 This doctoral thesis at the University of Ghent in 1985, over which professor Helmut Gaus presided, has not been published.

of anxiety. As virtually all textbooks of art history observe, one of the typical characteristics of these so-called romantic phases is precisely the increased emotional quality of paintings, music, literature, etc. That these phases coincided, especially in the nineteenth century but also now, with the descending Kondratievs is again an indication that the general hypothesis is correct. It thus is possible to predict that from now on, during the new ascending conjunctural phase, all forms of art will evolve towards a new and constantly renewing rationality, with the incorporation of all the formal characteristics which these movements have always displayed. It must be clear that art movements are never precisely to be pinpointed in time: there are always precursors, and some art branches continue for a very long time along the once chosen path (e.g. the romantic paintings of the nineteenth century). An additional problem for further research along these lines is the increasing divergence of art movements and schools, as we get closer to our own time.

6. The changing significance of the past

It is not immediately obvious that an increase in the average level of basic anxiety in society also changes the relation to the past and thus to history. If we apply the general theory, the argument runs that the interest in the past and history increases in parallel with the increase in basic anxiety because this interest in the past — or the past itself — acquires a function within the mechanism for fending off anxiety.

This very complex psychological mechanism can be clarified as follows. Insecurity and basic anxiety imply above all uncertainty about one's own identity, expressed in the question: "Who am I?" And automatically the following question arises: "Where do I come from?" Hence, the dimension of the past suddenly becomes relevant and significant again, be it on an emotional rather than a rational level. For the seeker of identity, the past presents itself as an instrument capable of diminishing latent insecurity in general, and thus the insecurity about one's identity in particular. In other words, one goes in search of one's "roots".

That this interest in the past is so widespread in the 1970s, and in particular in the 1980s, that the preoccupation with the past has sustained itself for so many years, indicates that the anxiety reduction function of the past operates fairly efficiently. The concept of "roots" which, in the last few

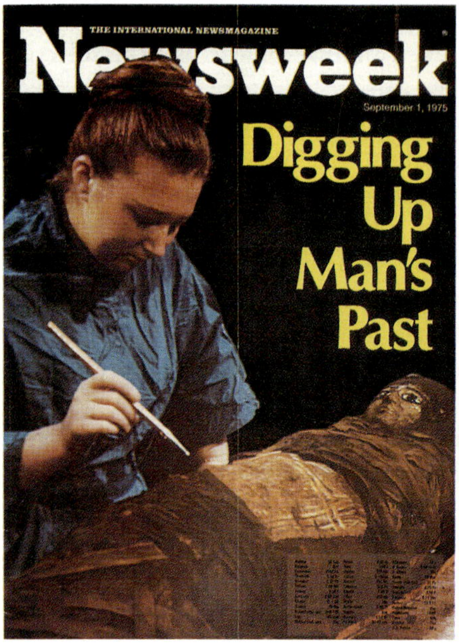

Illustration 6.5: 01-09-1975

Illustration 6.6: 1996, 44

years and also in non-English communities, has become a fashionable shorthand for the quest for the origins of someone's identity, not only restricts its common meaning to the realm of the past, namely the past of one's family, the particular social group, or one's people; the notion also very clearly indicates the emotive character of this disposition towards the past. It is no coincidence that this search for the past, for a history of the people, the land or the village, is an essential part of the propaganda of nationalist and extreme right-wing movements. The latter flourish especially during the descending periods and the lowest points of the long wave, hence in periods during which individuals become increasingly insecure of themselves.

The essence of the anxiety reduction mechanism is that, as insecurity in the present about ourselves and thus about the rest of the world increases, we turn to the past as an escape from the present. Everything in that past (which we also reconstruct to satisfy those needs) thereby obtains a positive emotional colouring.

As the past has many facets, there are many terrains in which this renewed interest in the past can manifest itself. There is, for instance, the historical novel (typical of the romantic period), in addition to historical fiction in the cinema and on television, the interest in retro in general and in grandmother's time in particular, the interest in antiques, museums and monuments, the blossoming of archaeology. If historiography itself would ideally follow the fluctuation of the long waves of basic anxiety, it can be expected that a more rational socio-scientific movement, such as the school of the *Annales*, would gain in importance during the descending phases of the long wave of anxiety (as was the case during the Sixties and at the beginning of the Seventies), whereas the more narrative historiography would be typical of the ascending phases (from the Seventies to the present). In other words, the long waves of anxiety define the confrontation between history as science and history as art. In the case of archaeology, where roots are literally searched for with the spade in hand, it has sufficiently been demonstrated that its flourishing coincides with the low-point periods of the long wave, which generally also witness strong nationalism. Here as well, however, further quantitative research is required.[4] In order to define the interest in antiques, and its correlation with the theory of the long waves of basic anxiety, an answer must be sought to the question whether antique prices have indeed risen in the last twenty years. If that is the case, a gradual decline can be expected over the coming decades. Further questions to be considered relate to the market in a more distant past: what share, for instance, do historical novels occupy in the total book production of the last two decades? Is there a fluctuation to be observed in government allocations for the renovation of historical buildings, for the maintenance of monuments and museums? In the case of the latter, it is clear that politicians are very sensitive to the financing of projects appreciated by the broader public. Since these financial decisions are taken in the descending period of a long wave, in which serious savings are usually necessary, even the status quo of the "historical" budget must be considered to be an increase.

In the new rationality of the ascending conjunctural wave, history is gradually once more becoming associated with the old-fashioned and the internal admiration for the past fades away. There is no more basic anxiety and thus no longer a need for "roots". In the 1950s and 1960s, for instance, there was little general interest in history. What is more, the general attitude of constantly growing confidence in one's abilities, capabilities and the future implied a condemnation of this type of interest as old-fashioned: in fact, the past in itself was divested of its value. It is clear, however, that, despite this change in mentality, grand projects, institutions or renovations that were decided upon during the descending phase, cannot

4 Important elements can be found in Margarita Diaz-Andreu & Timothy Champion, eds., *Nationalism and Archaeology in Europe*. London 1996.

suddenly be undone. They will continue to exist in society, but they will hold less significance for the broader public.

The interest, almost love, for the past is also — or ideally, should be — expressed in the number of historical manifestations, the success of historical memorials and societies or, more precisely, their growth in number, the increase of their members, and most importantly, the degree of participation in their activities. In addition, the interest in the past can be studied through the number of historical publications addressed to the lay public, such as the many Chronicles which swept the market a few years ago, but for which quantitative printing information is not available.

In the present context, local history deserves special attention as it engages with two of the components of anxiety behaviour which grow in strength with the descending of the long wave, namely the penchant for anything small-scale, for cocooning (see supra, section 1) on the one hand, and the fondness for the historical on the other.

The increased interest in historical fiction needs, of course, to be connected with the growing importance of fiction in general during a period of a long descending conjuncture; otherwise, historical fiction could not have taken such a flight. Section 14 discusses in more detail the altered significance of fiction in the context of the long waves.

The positive emotional colouring and jolliness of the past can also be recognised in the "retro"- fashions in the most diverse fields. There is the interest in old forms of living and houses in which old beams are used, or bricks that are aged artificially. There are the restaurants that are only considered cosy if they give the impression of having been decorated a hundred years ago; beer is served which is brewed in the old craft traditions and the bread preferably does not in any way resemble a white wheat loaf. Supported by the authority of dieticians who explain that the wholemeal bread has a much higher nutritional value than that of ordinary white bread, one is eager to believe and participate in this particular enhancement of the past.

The fondness for the past is also illustrated by the special interest in all things antique: antique furniture, photographs of ancestors in an antique frame, a Jugendstil lamp, an open fireplace which can devour mighty blocks of wood, chairs with cane seats, or leather, or artificial leather which looks like the real thing — for leather is the past and plastic is today.

The past, moreover, inspires new products: new furniture is for sale which, without attempting to hide it, imitates the furniture to be found in a more distant past in the houses of newly affluent farmers: massive, heavy, skilfully turned oak tables and cupboards which have defied centuries, and now carry for the potential buyer the impression of constancy and solidity. If one then questions the origins of the admiration for this combination of solidity, sturdiness, and not too refined artiness, or more precisely, if one examines the psychological background against which all this receives a positive evaluation, the synchronicity of this evolution in taste with the ascending phase of the long wave of anxiety suggests a causal relation with the increasing insecurity and anxiety of the buying public.

The rituals accompanying marriage constitute (here) a final example of the past as a source of inspiration for the present. After the rationality, and even materialism, of the Sixties, which from the vantage point of the present psychological context is experienced as dull and boring, catalogues suddenly appeared once more full of white lace bridal gowns, which suggested earlier marriage romanticism, and which grew in success as the divorce rate rose sky-high. The general insecurity and basic anxiety clearly also affected the perspectives and durability of marriage, and it is precisely the altered perception of marriage — and not the divorce rates — which gave the earlier lace bridal gowns a new lease on life: they offer a kind of ritual exorcism of the anxiety.

7. Feminism and sexuality

It is, of course, hazardous for a non-psychologist to approach the extremely complex matter of the influence of growing or decreasing anxiety on sexuality. Many interviews, tests and case studies are available. However, there appears to be no psychological study that pays attention to the impact of the long waves on the experience of sexuality and the position of the woman in society. That the long waves have a quite significant effect on the women's liberation movement and sexuality is already suggested by the evolution of the longitudinal trends in fashion and the discussion of the family in section 1, and the analysis of the changing marriage rituals in section 6.

We have seen that, at the peaks of the long wave of conjuncture, hence during the periods of little basic anxiety and great security, fashion contributes to the image of women who have clearly distanced themselves from the historically grown, typically female role patterns, and who strive

Illustration 6.7: 23-03-1970

for an effective, rational recognition of their equality with men. It is important to recognise the additional implication, namely that men themselves are to an increasing degree receptive to such aspirations, and that they no longer inspire them with fear. During the ascending period of the long wave and in particular at its peak, sexuality has become something evident and normal — which is not to say that it has become banal. This is the flourishing period of the liberation movement of women, the mentality of the *soixante-huitards* at its prime: sexuality exists, but there is no reason to treat it with mystery or in an underhand manner. Sexuality is satisfactory and therefore without problems. This also explains why the miniskirt of the Seventies was in those years not seen as sexually provocative — something which the majority of people, now confronted with it, do experience. Moreover, all other characteristics of the miniskirt were clearly non-sexual. It is important to realise that the current mood at the lowest point of the long wave risks inspiring a false interpretation for a number of cultural phenomena that flourished at the peak of the conjuncture.

For the last curve in the long wave, then, the most pressing problem in this context is the degree to which the increase in basic anxiety and insecurity alters the complex system of relationships. Expressed in ideal-typical terms:

Graph 6.6: Number of summer dresses with low neckline, 1956 – 2000

Per annum and 9-year moving averages
Source: Libelle, Rijk der Vrouw, Flair

the woman who becomes more and more insecure and anxious no longer wishes to be "liberated" and feels safer in her former role pattern; if the more anxious man were to be confronted with a "liberated" woman, his feeling of insecurity would be sharpened, but this is not the case because he is restored to his former role of the father. In short, the return to the former role models and the exertion to push one another into those patterns permits a more comfortable relationship.

One conclusion on this complex subject matter can thus be stated without reservation: when insecurity and anxiety increase (during the descending phase of the long wave of conjuncture), the partner relationship, possibly within a family, acquires a supplementary function, namely the reduction of basic anxiety — as was already stated in section 1.

We may also assume that sexuality contributes greatly to the strength of a relationship. As the relation becomes more important because of its role in the reduction of basic anxiety, sexuality also increases in importance. However, sexuality thereby acquires an unnatural function: it also has to tie the partner because s/he plays a role in the anxiety reduction, and not solely because s/he is loved. That is not the function of sexuality, or more accurately, it can in fact not carry the extra taxation. Sex therefore increasingly becomes less satisfying, yields less pleasure and has a less liberating effect. As a further result, sexuality becomes more problematic, and one becomes more conscious of it. Many will therefore go in search of alternative forms of sexuality from which they hope to receive more enjoyment. Logically this has to result in a certain percentage of adherents of pornography and other indirect forms of sexuality. The correlation with the long wave is once more confirmed if one compares the contemporary trend in the latter with the situation thirty years ago, at the time of the miniskirt and unisex hairstyles.

Therefore, with the ascending long wave ahead of us, we can foretell a long period of women's liberation. In fact, all that has happened in this field before has been the onset of a long upward trend that will continue for many years and become stronger. The repercussion it will have on traditional family life will not be quite important.

8. The transformation of basic anxiety into fear: the search for catastrophes[5]

This section is based on a psychological mechanism developed by a number of authors and which can best be described as the transformation of basic anxiety into fear. The former refers to a vague, diffuse feeling of anxiety, without it being projected on to an actual situation or actual persons. Perhaps its meaning is best illustrated by the American phrase "free floating anxiety". The term "fear", on the other hand, refers to anxiety inspired by a concrete situation, concrete people or things. The psychological mechanism of the transmutation of anxiety into fear is based on the understanding that the psyche itself has a very specific reason for its tendency to transform anxiety into fear. For anxiety is a vague feeling that has a paralysing effect

5 See also chapter 3, under: *Different kinds of anxiety.*

Illustration 6.8: 1986, 33

Illustration 6.9: 26-04-1982

Illustration 6.10: 1982, 13

Illustration 6.11: 1993, 26

on our behaviour, that tampers with the easy course of our everyday tasks, precisely because it continuously demands our attention. Fear, on the other hand, is only experienced in confrontation with the fear-inspiring situation, people or things. Without confrontation, there is no fear.

Anxious people, who are searching for something to be fearful of, are in fact seeking to get rid of their anxiety by transforming it into fear. In a descending phase of the long wave, basic anxiety and insecurity will increase among a great number of people in society. The psychological mechanism will be activated and many will eagerly search for something to project their anxiety on to. It is evident that the media quickly accommodate the growing need for "fearful things". Although they do not know the reasons, they understand that there is virtually no limit to the provision of alarmist information on the threatening situation of the ozone layer, the greenhouse effect, the destruction of fauna and flora through disasters with oil tankers, the extinction of the species, AIDS, Ebola and other mysterious diseases, nuclear winters and any other catastrophes which may cause the destruction of the world. In short, "doom and gloom" is really "in" and functional.

A few examples illustrate the point. The second half of the twentieth century experienced the Cold War between East and West, and it is well known how the arms race in the West was fuelled by the fear for the USSR. That fear was uncritically adopted by the population, which enabled Western governments to spend inconceivable sums of money on armament without being challenged or criticised. The difference in protest, for instance, against the Vietnam War between the years before 1970 and the years after 1970, clearly indicates how the climate had changed. A quantitative comparison of participants in the peace movements before and after 1970 would equally be relevant. Finally, it is probable that a systematic study of the frequency of fear-inducing covers of popular magazines in the different countries of the West is a good parameter for the measurement of the gradation in intensity and frequency of this shift from anxiety to fear. Indeed, all the covers of the German weekly *Der Spiegel* on which the words "Angst" appeared date from the end of the Eighties and the beginning of the Nineties.

The success of nature movements and green parties in periods of descending conjuncture is partly due to the same psychological mechanism. They also profit from the heightened degree of emotionality (section 5), which contributes to their romantic appeal, because they are perceived to offer a strong affective bond with nature. When the heightened emotionality disappears and the mechanism of the transformation of anxiety into fear weakens, that affectivity will disappear from the nature movement. What

Illustration 6.12: 1986, 20

Illustration 6.13: 1987, 11

Illustration 6.14: 1987, 1

Illustration 6.15: 1987, 47

will remain are only the warnings about the real threats to nature, but they will be much less able to alarm greater parts of the population, and to inspire them to caution and protest. In this respect, the historical wave movements in the interest in nature in literature, paintings, philosophy, etc., deserve closer scrutiny. We will return to the meaning of nature in greater detail in section 17.

In short, it can be argued that descending conjunctural waves and low periods create an optimal climate for all types of doom merchants and calamity bringers. During the ascending waves, on the other hand, the masses sometimes express a stupefying indifference with regard to genuinely threatening situations, because the need to transform anxiety into fear has faded. More particularly, there ought to be a clear difference between the period 1950-1970, in which, according to the present theory, the fear for disasters and catastrophes would be only present in a limited way, and the period 1970-1990, where a great increase in that fear would be noticeable — quite apart from the realistically possible threats. Today we may state that this fear is gradually declining, although in real terms the dangers may well be increasing considerably. The factual situation, however, will not be able to rally the necessary interest.

9. The changing fear of death

A very specific case of the transformation of anxiety into fear relates to death. Apart from the many catastrophes mentioned in the previous section, the heightened basic anxiety also seeks to transform itself into the fear of death. This implies that death can also function as a possible catastrophe. That is to say, in an ascending phase of the long conjunctural wave, the fear of death is relatively low, but it increases in conjunction with the decline of the long wave; in the descending phase of the Nineties fear of death reaches its highest point but is gradually decreasing since. This will drastically change the mentality of large sections of the population, in the matter of death as well life — the other side of the coin — and everything connected with it. Unsafe behaviour such as smoking among young people will increase. Advertising that should be conductive to health — such as mentioning that the product does not contain sugar, or no or very little fats, or that they are "light" — will lose its appeal.

The conception of this phenomenon is informed by the understanding that, with increased anxiety, self-preoccupation and emotionality also grow. Death, not unlike any other possible catastrophe, comes to be more related to the Ego and is approached more emotionally; it acquires a certain veil of mystery once more. That the receptivity for the issue of death has increased dramatically emerges again from the covers of popular magazines in the West since the 1970s, with editors recognising the increased attention to this theme.

The study of J. Sevens also provides important confirmation of the hypothesis. On the basis of bookshop catalogues from three Western countries, Sevens studied the frequency of published titles on death and related subjects. With the understanding that the book market is susceptible to public demand, he noted — over a long-term period — an effective rise and decline in the number of the titles on death. The most remarkable conclusion of this study is the fact that the years with the highest number of titles were precisely the lowest points of the Kondratiev waves. The questions on aetiology that arise because of that synchronism cannot be discussed within the scope of the present paper. But this longitudinal research is evidently equally important in demonstrating the hypothesis.

In the middle of the 1990s, it is difficult to conceive the attitude towards death in ascending periods of the conjunctural wave, when basic anxiety declines. In general terms, death will then be perceived as something obvious and natural, something that will occur and is not worth worrying about, something which does not warrant excessive fear. And this can perhaps explain a fact which many have already noted, namely that all great wars in the West have taken place in the ascending periods or at the peaks of the long wave, i.e. in periods of little basic anxiety. In the first peak period, the Napoleonic wars took place; in the second ascending phase, the wars of Bismarck and the Franco-German war; in the third ascending period, the First World War; and in the fourth, the Second World War. Conversely, no major wars have been fought in any of the descending periods. In conjunction with the above, it is evidently difficult to imagine that soldiers, during a descending conjunctural wave, would depart for the front smiling, singing and full of enthusiasm — something which is conceivable in an ascending period with its low levels of anxiety and fear, and which has effectively happened.

In this context, the average contempt for death would be the direct consequence of the level of the average basic anxiety in society, and thus the determining factor for the readiness of the masses to fight. The evolution of the attitude in the USA with regard to the Vietnam War is once again a particularly striking example. It has to be noted, however, that the readiness to fight cannot be equated with aggression (the latter will be discussed in section 13).

Illustration 6.16: 1993, 6

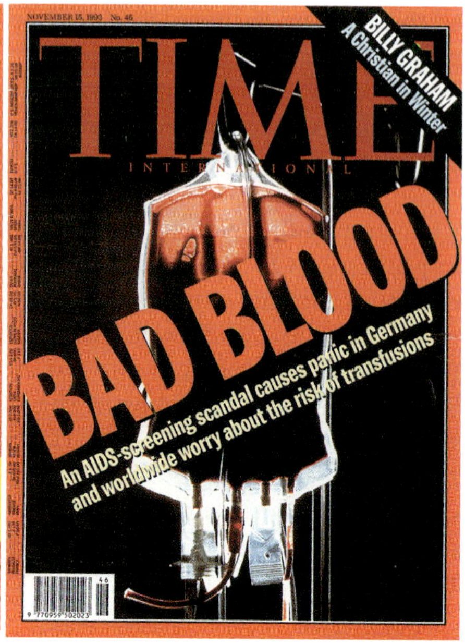

Illustration 6.17: 1993, 46

In psychological terms, it is obvious that with the increased fear of death, the preoccupation with life, and thus health, also increases. With reference to the last half of this century, this would imply that in the period from the 1970s to today, the general concern about health is much higher than in the 1950s and 1960s. Around 1970, the tide must have been on the turn, with the concern with health turning more emotional and more related to the Ego. Although quantitative data on the growth of the health industry are clearly relevant, they must be employed with the necessary caution, for the same period has witnessed an important rise in living standards, the aging of the population and thus a growth of the infirm — all factors with obvious consequences for the health industry. The heightening of the emotional, egocentric preoccupation with health may, arguably, be confirmed more by the increase in fitness clubs, diet concerns and the attention to health in newspapers and magazines (indicated by the percentage of space allotted to the subject), by the concern for the body and all kinds of health publications; in short, by the growth of the health industry as a whole.

The growing concern for health is clearly not solely the direct consequence of the fear of death. It also involves an element which would best be judged by the medical profession, but which can be described as follows. As a

Illustration 6.18: 1985, 39

Illustration 6.19: 1997, 21

result of increasing insecurity and anxiety, everyday activities, whether professional or personal, come to be far more taxing than they had been during the rather carefree ascending period of the long wave. Hence, the same activities, the same problems, are much more stressful and pathogenic in the descending phase. And that also explains in part the increasing preoccupation with health.

Research in this area should equally include magic-mythical healing practices: it is precisely in periods of increasing insecurity, higher emotionality and higher egocentrism, that they possess a far greater attractiveness than in the ascending phase of the long wave, when the pragmatic, sober and rational spirit dominates. Section 15 will return to the magic-mythical dimension in more detail.

The hypothesis, however, already suggests that, apart from linear, i.e. non-conjunctural evolutions (such as the increase of the third age, the growing number of the infirm etc.), the growing indifference towards death during the ascending phase of the long wave will cause a relative decline in medical consumption.

10. Motility

Motility, derived from the Latin verb *movere*, to move, is here taken to express the inclination anxious people have to keep moving, to do something, to keep busy; for its opposite, simply not doing anything, not being busy, is a situation in which one experiences one's anxiety and uncertainty at their strongest. Motility as a means of anxiety reduction is well known in the psychology of individuals. The question then arises as to whether this phenomenon can also be found in the masses during a descending conjuncture wave. It is, in fact, precisely since 1971 that in the Western countries, ramblers' movements have started emerging. Clubs were formed in order to walk together for miles and miles, something that would have been completely unthinkable three years earlier, that is, in May 1968. It must also be noted that these movements (including cycling clubs) have since continued to increase their membership and have organised an increasing number of activities. At the beginning of the 1920s, that is, immediately after the beginning of the decline of the Kondratiev, C.G. Jung remarked on a similar phenomenon, which he saw as accompanying the manifestation of the Wodan archetype, which is usually marked by great acts of violence. The emergence of Fascism has confirmed this. However, our unfamiliarity with the theory of archetypes does not allow us to adopt Jung's model of interpretation in the present context.

Illustration 6.20: 1985, 22

Illustration 6.21: 1980, 19

The flourishing of hobby clubs and in particular DIY-firms is, arguably, another phenomenon which can equally be interpreted as an expression of that need for motility as a consequence of the increasing uncertainty and anxiety. It is evident that a whole range of other, perhaps even stronger, factors are equally responsible for the flourishing of this type of firm, such as thriftiness for instance. In the last analysis, however, I maintain that someone's inclination to repair a sink or bicycle themselves is in part determined by the average level of societal anxiety. The use of bicycles, especially by people who are not forced (by necessity or thrift) to use them, can possibly be used as a yardstick. Here as well, a longitudinal study would offer more information. In essence, what is under investigation is the socio-cultural translation of the restlessness of the anxious person. Prima facie, this involves mostly rather trivial things, but it is clear that the presence and evolution of the average societal anxiety can reveal itself through the analysis of trivial, everyday things and events.

To what extent travelling and tourism should also be viewed from this standpoint is an open question since travelling can be seen as an escapist but also as an expansive impulse which is typical for an ascending conjuncture.

11. Status and prestige in relation to the hiding of uncertainty

The ambition for status and prestige is intrinsic to most people and characteristic to all times. The reasons why people appreciate the building of a certain image for themselves and others is a very complex matter, which responds to many sociological and psychological functions. The search and striving for a certain status and prestige can be expressed through many aspects of everyday life. A few examples will suffice: fashion (a particular label for instance, or a particular tailor), interior decoration (the style, the quantity of antiques, carpets, paintings) architecture (including the ownership of swimming pools, tennis courts, and at a certain moment in Germany, even individual nuclear shelters), the organisation of the work place, communication (the importance of letterheads, logos), etc.

In essence, the ambition of the people who equip themselves with these prestige and status symbols is always the acquisition of surplus value for themselves. The search for this surplus value is at least in part connected with a feeling of inferiority, and it is precisely here that the phenomenon provides a link with the long waves. For if we accept that uncertainty and anxiety increase with the decline of the long waves and that, in this movement, the individual becomes a problem for themselves, this then immediately implies the forceful necessity not to show this, or conversely, the necessity to present oneself as better (stronger, more powerful) than one actually feels in relation to a third party. At the peaks of the long waves, in which the feeling of self-confidence dominates, one simply is what one is: a strong ego. There is nothing to hide and nothing to simulate. Status and prestige, in fact, are regarded as rather immature. They may be present, but certainly not ostentatiously so.

Illustration 6.22: 1986, 48

Illustration 6.23: 14-07-1975

This increase in the importance of status and prestige in a descending phase of the long wave, i.e. an ascending phase of the wave of anxiety, is obviously connected with the feeling, mentioned above, of individualism, or, more accurately, egocentrism. For the latter increases in emphasis and visibility through the increased importance of status and prestige. From this increased importance, it also follows that the differences in status and prestige are much more sharply experienced. In plain words: at the peak of a long wave, a ingenious idea on a scrap of paper is regarded as a ingenious idea; at the lowest point of the long wave, a ingenious idea on a scrap of paper is regarded as a scrap of paper. The impact of formalities is then at its highest and this clearly has far-reaching consequences for the formal design and packing of consumer products.

Regarded as a methodological problem, it is difficult, however, to find longitudinal series of behaviour, which mirror the evolution of the importance of status and prestige. One possibility could be the design of bodywork for motorcars. During the last twenty years, there has not been a single design which did not, in one way or another, radiate status and prestige. Cars which were intentionally and exclusively designed as efficient transport vehicles, without any attention to status or prestige, such as the Citroën 2CV, almost entirely disappeared from the streets after 1970. The first new car whose ambition was in the first place to look playful, and not prestigious, was the Mazda 121 in 1991. Playfulness is not appreciated by uncertain people. The successful sales rates of this model, and its successors from other manufacturers, appear to be a good parameter by which to conclude that we have started to leave the present lowest point of the long wave.

Perhaps it is also possible to study over a long period the percentage of everyday expenses that is spent on status and prestige.

12. Norms and values

Within society, there is a whole range of norms and values in operation that constantly organise and regulate people's communal life. And it must have occurred to most people of a certain age that there are periods in which these norms and values are relatively unproblematic, in the sense that virtually nobody contemplates them for any length of time, or more strongly, that they are a preoccupation only in the sense that what is experienced as a straitjacket is contested. This contestation itself, however, will never inspire anyone to re-evoke the doom-mongering images of decadence. This period constitutes what has come to be called the "permissive society", seen in the West at the end of the 1960s and at the beginning of the 1970s — when yellow, red and orange miniskirts dominated the street image.

In sharp contrast there is the great importance attached to values nowadays. Since the beginning of the 1970s there has been a gradual emergence of a number of academic writings on values; today it has become a totally unsurveyable tide. However, these volumes do not provide a (detailed) answer to the question as to why values have become so important in the last two decades, whereas before they only received obligatory attention.

The same goes for the importance of norms that regulate our behaviour. In past periods, they were published in "books of etiquette", in which one could read how to behave at the dinner table, what to say on meeting a friend, which present to take to the hospital, etc. Many popular weekly and monthly magazines now have columns that fulfil the function of those etiquette booklets.

On a different level, norms and values also perform an important function for behaviour, including the behaviour of the more insecure individual in the long descending wave of 1970-1990. It is clear that, if one is uncertain because of the increase in the average societal anxiety level, one also becomes more uncertain in one's behaviour, both towards oneself and towards others. The knowledge of the dominant norms and values thus comes to be an important instrument to guide one's behaviour. This is how the dominant norms and values obtain their surplus value: they come to represent something that ought to be respected. In a period at the peak of the long wave of conjuncture, on the other hand, norms and values are not considered that valuable: one behaves as one sees fit, and that is generally accepted. Respect for norms and values is, at that point, seen rather as an obstacle, as a conservative reflex impeding the adaptation to progress. It is also possible to describe the change in attitude towards norms and values as an increase or decrease in the authority attributed to norms and values. The degree to which more people who are uncertain have an increasing need for authority, has already been indicated in section 2. The increasing importance ascribed to the past, as described in section 6, equally forms a close connection with the topic presently under discussion.

In methodological terms, again, it is not easy to find longitudinal information, which allows the definition of the increasing or decreasing respect for norms over a period longer than one century. Perhaps an accurate quantitative study of the importance given in the media to the negation of existing norms and values by prominent, mainly political, public figures can offer some results. In other words, it can be argued that the *scandalitis*, the recent great interest among the masses in political scandals, is an expression of the need for respected norms and values, characteristic of a time of increased uncertainty and anxiety. To put it more strongly: it is not the nature nor the frequency of important infringements of norms and values that determine whether they become headline news and occupy public opinion for a long time; rather, it is the strength of the awareness of norms and values among this public, which itself is in part influenced by the long waves. This argument implies that our time, as much as the 1930s and 1990s, is a flourishing period of *scandalitis*. The evidence in the Western European context is clear: at the lowest point of the long wave at the end of the last century, France experienced the Dreyfus affair that mesmerised the whole of the population for years. At the lowest point of the 1930s, again in France, there was the Stavisky affair. To realise the degree to which our own time is one of political and other scandals, it is sufficient to follow the news.

But a systematic study is desirable in order to test the verity of the hypothesis put forward. Some indications could be obtained, for instance, by a systematic longitudinal study of the place and importance of traditional norms and values in party political programmes or electoral manifestos.

13. The aggression of the cornered rat

With the question of the impact of the average level of basic anxiety on aggression, we probably have reached one of the most difficult sections of this paper. There are two reasons why the section is retained nonetheless. In section 9 it has been argued that in the Western context, wars have always occurred in an ascending conjuncture, a period with mass readiness for war, when one left singing to the front. On the other hand, the study by A. Fordyn (1981) informs us that, since the middle of the nineteenth century, the frequency of terrorist attacks in Western Europe always increases in the lowest points of the long conjunctural waves, that is, contemporary with the increase in uncertainty and fear, whereas the attacks decrease towards the peaks of the long waves. The problem then becomes one of reconciling these diverse elements and of establishing the precise role of increasing or diminishing anxiety with regard to aggression.

Although the literature on aggression among the masses is extremely limited, the following hypothesis can be put forward. First, however, it is important to note the distinction between two forms of aggression, that is, to distinguish between defensive and offensive aggression, or metaphorically, between the aggression of the rat which, driven into a corner, attacks, or that of the cat in its hunt for mice. The defensive form of aggression dominates during an increase in uncertainty and anxiety; offensive aggression dominates when basic anxiety is virtually absent.

It is clear that increasing uncertainty in a descending phase of the long wave also causes a feeling of powerlessness in the individual who withdraws into themselves, becomes preoccupied with their pain and experiences all of this in a strongly emotional manner. At the same time, society as a whole (the institutions, the city, the humanly constructed world) is experienced as an unalterable fact. When the suppressed anxiety, generally known to be the other side of the coin, turns into aggression, it is not unlike the lid that flies off the kettle when the pressure grows too high. Alternatively, for certain people, defensive aggression offers relief from suppressed uncertainty and anxiety. The direction of this aggression, its motivation, and other similarly rational considerations, are problems and questions that only emerge after the event; and their answers depend upon the cultural, social and political climate. The latter constitutes the cloak for what can be called defensive aggression. At the low point of the 1890s, this type of aggression manifested itself in a whole series of terrorist attacks against monarchs. The study of the political climate of that time, and in particular the antimonarchical socialist propaganda, renders those events virtually self-explanatory. But terrorism returned, even when there were no longer any monarchs. In short, this type of aggression fades away with the ascent of the long conjunctural wave as has been described by Fordyn. Here, it is argued that in the last analysis, this type of aggression fades away because the basic anxiety fades away.

Illustration 6.24: 1986, 39

Illustration 6.25: 1990, 46

Offensive aggression then is the exact opposite. In a rather primitive phrase, it can be described as the aggression motivated by the experience of lust — in the way that children can be destructive simply because they like it, and not because they are anxious or hope to find relief. No negative feelings need to be vented. One can be invited to engage in offensive aggression by others, by an ideology, by the occasion, by flags. Offensive aggression is experienced as a positive feeling and it is preferably experienced in a group. Defensive aggression, on the contrary, is experienced as grim defiance or as a bitter act of resistance and it is preferably experienced by oneself.

The above distinction makes it abundantly clear why in ascending phases of the long wave of anxiety terrorist attacks and similar kinds of aggression increase, while the receptivity to offensive aggression feeds the hunger for war from the soldier to the general. Aggression at school as depicted in the film *The Blackboard Jungle* (1955) is evidently offensive aggression. This was also the case with the May 1968 student revolt in Paris and many other university towns. In an ascending phase of the long wave, the latter is accompanied by the decrease in the need and the respect for authority: it can therefore take much more powerful and violent forms, and ultimately, by its mass character, becomes much more dangerous and undermining for the legitimate authority.

14. To live in fictional worlds

It is important here first to clarify the terms. What we are concerned with are not fictitious worlds; but fictional worlds, that is, the world of novels or films, which are, during the reading or viewing, really present — be it that these real worlds consist of imagined, fictional material. In addition, it is important to identify the three research angles offered by the interaction between the evolution of the imagination and the evolution of the long waves: first, the quantitative evolution of the consumption of fiction; secondly, the evolution in the fictionalisation of reality; and finally, the evolution in the content of fiction.

According to the material already gathered, the descending period of a long wave, with its increasing uncertainty and anxiety, is also characterised by the increasing consumption of fiction (film, literature, cartoons, etc.) It is relatively straightrforward to explain this characteristic of the quantitative evolution in the consumption of fiction: in the descending periods of the long wave, the *hic et nunc*, the here and now, are not periods of joy, of positive attitudes and self-content, which one wants to enjoy as long as possible and in which one wants to stay as long as possible. This is, on the contrary, the case during ascending periods of the long wave, especially the peak periods. In the former case, it is a self-evident reflex to live, as far as possible, in other worlds, the worlds of the imagination. What is involved here is the well-known "escapism", the flight, for the duration of a film or a novel, from the world in which one lives.

It is important to acknowledge here that this evolution in the consumption of fiction has also been perceived in periods that are not connected with the long waves. In societies that, because of the political regime for instance, have reached unyielding stagnation, in which individuals no longer have the impression they can do anything, the consumption of fiction increases. Witnesses have testified to the inconceivable decrease of the consumption of fiction concurrent with the fall of the old USSR under Gorbatchev, the moment when people again had the impression that they could take their fate into their own hands. But this example does not contradict the hypothesis. On the contrary, it indicates the likeliness of this mechanism also coming into play when the world becomes more sombre during a descending phase of the long wave. In the degree to which it is influenced by the long wave, it will also mirror an increase or decrease of fiction.

With the fictionalisation of reality, a subtler problem is at issue. Prima facie, there is no problem: everyone knows the difference between real and fictional worlds. At closer sight, however, our perception of reality, which evidently always includes an interpretation of this reality, is much more entangled with our imagination than is generally acknowledged. An example: a Muslim fundamentalist, an average Western person and a former communist hold very different perceptions of the everyday world, not because the everyday things are different, but because those things are placed in a different perspective by an act of imagination. Alternatively, if we consider the everyday world of an average Nazi in 1930s Germany: for that German, the inferiority of the Jews, the ingenious Führer, the submission of the woman, etc., are components of the real world. To label this as fictitious is to deny reality. Popular belief is also a fertile domain for the study of the fictionalisation of reality: devils, spirits, bad omens, etc. belonged to these people's reality.

In particular with regard to the last example, the question may arise as to its relation with the argument which presents the evolution of humankind as a whole as a great de-fictionalisation of reality, and which denominates the contemporary phase as one of secularisation. The present context clearly does not allow for further investigation of such wide and difficult issues.

What remains to be considered, however, is whether we can maintain that the lowest-point periods of the last three long waves, that is, the 1890s, the 1930s and the contemporary period, are indeed periods characterised by a higher degree of the fictionalisation of reality? There is no question that during the 1890s the socialist vision and during the 1930s the Fascist vision coloured the perception of reality to a very high degree. Perhaps the problem lies with the contemporary vision of reality: where is the fictionalisation here? It is argued here that relatively soon after the start of the decline of the long wave, around 1970, we were confronted with the fictionalisation of nature, expressed, among others, in the many green parties which emerged everywhere in the West. The effect of an increasing feeling of anxiety and uncertainty regarding the perception of nature will be discussed in section 17.

The third aspect to be considered here is the longitudinal influence of increasing or decreasing anxiety on the content of fiction, and more specifically, especially since the 1920s, on the content of films. Three elements stand out here. To begin, it was in the 1970s that the first demonological films appeared. They had existed before that time but they had led a rather modest existence in the margins of the general evolution. They mostly took the form of rather monotonous vampire films, with often the same, mostly English, actors. Only with *Rosemary's Baby* (1968) did the demonic emerge in a totally new form. More accurately, this film was a forerunner and the fact that it was very successful demonstrates that a new sensibility for this type of fiction was about to be born. For numerous films since (sometimes within a science-fiction setting), the diabolical and the demonic have procured box office successes.

The second aspect that has become much more prominent since the increase of basic uncertainty and anxiety from the 1970s onwards, is the showing of cruel scenes. In this respect, the bloody spaghetti westerns were the forerunners. The realism of gruesomeness has since reached an excellence which has provoked considerable protest against horror films such as *The Texas Chainsaw Massacre* (1974). It was feared that through some kind of imitation effect, this type of extremely violent film could be the cause of the increase of cruelty and criminality in society.

A final fundamental change in the content of films is documented by a study of the mostly American success films of the 1930s. It emerged that in the dramatic films, until circa 1933, the fateful situation in which the protagonists found themselves had been caused by others, so that resistance to the situation (in whatever form, and irrespective of its success) was workable. After 1933, however, the fateful drama was caused by

Illustration 6.26: 1975, 9

Illustration 6.27: 21-11-1977

anonymous forces and circumstances against which human resistance was no longer possible. Research on the inter-war years has also shown that the darkening of the genre ran parallel with the bloom of a completely different genre, namely the operetta film in which reality as it existed outside the theatre was suppressed. More accurately perhaps, because of the reality outside the theatre, it was possible to be so euphorically, one-sidedly joyful. In more general terms, it may be argued that, as the real situation becomes more poignant and miserable, the receptivity for artificial escapist joy increases. Another example of this general argument can be found in the carnivals of the poor Latin-American states.

What then is the relation between, on the one hand, the increase in the demonic and the gruesome, and on the other the increase in the average level of basic anxiety in society?

First, it has to be noted that the consumption of fiction, whether written or visual, evolves according to the mechanisms of the market. No one is forced to consume a certain type of fiction, and one only consumes that fiction from which one expects much pleasure and relaxation. Therefore, if horror films are successful, it can be assumed that they respond to a general need. The question then must focus on what has changed in the mind so that demonic or gruesome fictional experiences are "relaxing". And the answer presented here is, again, that the increase of basic uncertainty and anxiety are responsible. There are historical parallels. Preachers never depicted the gruesomeness of hell so graphically and cruelly as in periods of cholera, Black Death and other long-lasting, precarious situations. These depictions were functional: the fictional cruelty was so extreme that the real cruelty, the reality, in the minds of the people, could only be a dull reproduction. In other words, the far worse fictional cruelty put the real situation into perspective. This example allows the extrapolation of the following general rule: the more terrifying the experience of the real situation, the more terrifying the fiction needs to be which is offered for consumption in order to put the real anxiety into perspective. The protest against fictional cruelty is therefore nonsensical. This does not imply the denial of the fact that it may inspire a small percentage of people to emulation, and thus to criminal behaviour. Its prohibition, however, does not solve the problem. This implies, conversely, that in a happy world, if that were to exist, this type of fiction is superfluous. In such a world, as Plato has already said, art is superfluous.

In methodological terms, research into film consumption along the lines sketched above is best based on a selection of films which are known to have been successful with the larger public. For periods further back in time, this study can only rely on popular literature.

The psychological conclusion then must be that the literature and fiction of the ascending conjuncture are of a very different nature. We no longer find the self-analysis, the self-observation and the navel-gazing, but rather the epic genre (which totally disappears in a descending phase of the long wave) as the best expression of the changing and changed spirit: at its centre is no longer the interest in oneself, but the interest in the other — the other human being, the other object, the other experience — and for that which is playful. That is a different section.

15. Irrationality and magic-mythical forms of thought

To define in an exhaustive manner what is meant by irrationality and magic-mythical forms of thought is beyond the scope of the present article. However, it is important to acknowledge that all our rationality is in part irrational and that magic-mythical thinking still pervades much of our everyday behaviour. Here, irrationality is taken to refer to an increased trust in astrology and paranormal sciences, in fortune-tellers and clairvoyants, in health-through-prayer, in lotteries, extraterrestrial visitors, telekinesis and, in a milder form, to the conviction that the human will is capable of anything. In its magic-mythical form, we refer to the increasing belief in mysterious forces, in devils (e.g. *Rosemary's Baby*), and, closely related, to a revival of the most diverse forms of popular belief and superstition such as apparitions, wondrous healing practices, and so forth. Numerous religious sects, of which many lead a dormant existence in the descending phase of the long wave of anxiety, reach, in a ascending phase, a far greater adherence and membership, precisely because irrationality and magic-mythical forms of thought have gained so considerably in trustworthiness. It must not be forgotten that only a small step back in the history of humankind leads to a world which was almost exclusively dominated by magic-mythical forms of thinking, that this type of thought is in fact as ancient as humankind itself.

Graph 6.7: The long wave of anxiety and the number of books on astrology in German and British libraries, 1955 – 2000

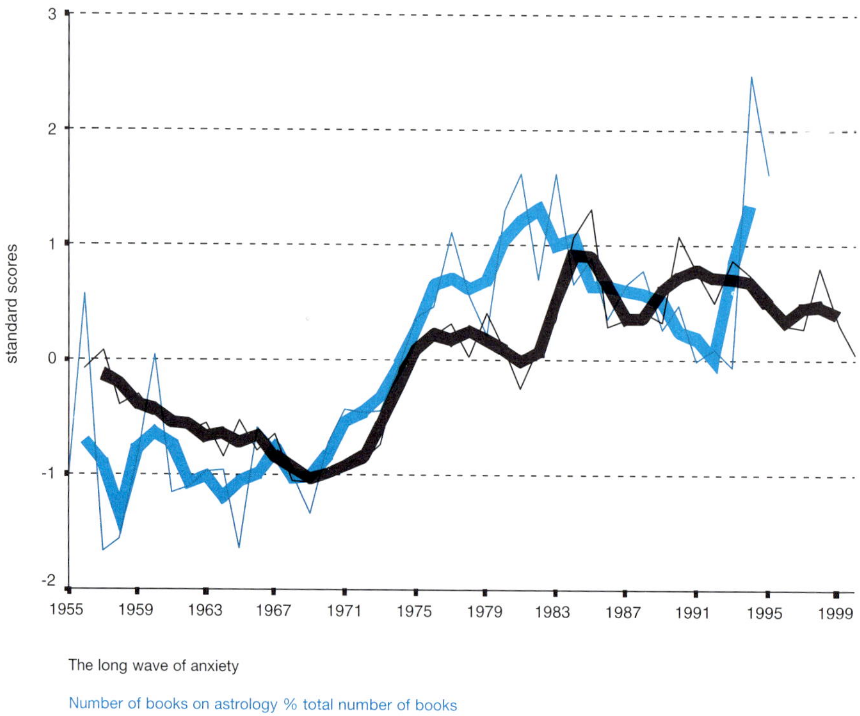

Per annum and 9-year moving averages
Source: Verbundkatalog (http://www.dbilink.de) and British Library (http://www.bl.uk) (OPAC 97))

Its suppression by rationality is fairly recent, and the de-fictionalisation of reality, as it has been called above, is still very much an incomplete process. In addition, the hypothesis presented here leads to the conclusion that this process in a descending conjuncture cycle undergoes a slight setback, a regression, as a result of the increased level of basic anxiety. The crowbar of reason and rationality looses its force because of the increased importance of emotion, and perhaps, in view of the former one-sidedness, this is not entirely undeserved. Anxiety is an emotion, and as it increases (the argument must be familiar by now), the whole field of perception and the patterns of reaction also become more emotional, at the expense of the rational, critical perception which dominates at the peaks of the long wave. The more emotional patterns of reaction are, by definition, more irrational.

Illustration 6.28: 1988, 6

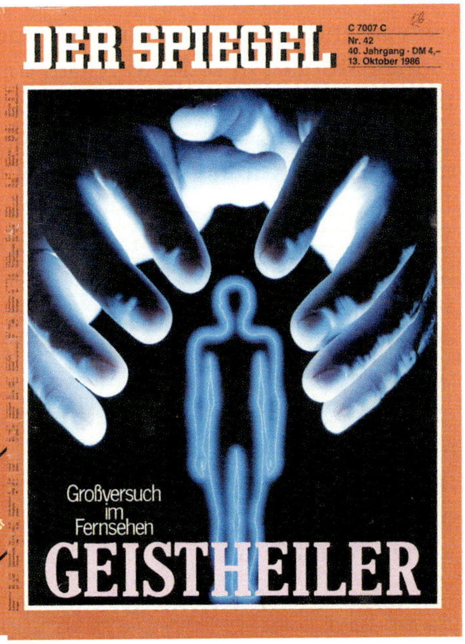

Illustration 6.29: 1986, 42

Lotteries, betting practices and their like are forms of irrational behaviour that testify to this part of the hypothesis. The belief that one has a chance of finding the needle in the haystack is clearly not very rational. But more important is the weight that is given to coincidence. In phases that testify to self-confidence in one's abilities and capacities, the mind is far less receptive to these gifts *ex absurdo*. What one achieves and acquires must be the result of one's own abilities and capacities, a conviction, which in its turn further strengthens the existing self-confidence. Conversely, as one has less (or fears to have less), the hope grows that coincidence may offer a helping hand. It is therefore logical to expect, in this respect too, the effect of the longitudinal increase of basic uncertainty. Although the available data point in the direction of the hypothesis, further historical research is, again, imperative.[6]

16. Anxiety deconstructs identity

This section is closely connected to section 3 in which the growth of egocentrism during the descending phases of the long wave was compared to the individualism at its peaks. Also, in section 6 we saw how individuals who are more and more uncertain increasingly invoke the help of the past, of their "roots", in order to regain some self-assertion. Here it is suggested that these more uncertain and, from necessity, more egocentric individuals face a fundamental problem with their own identity which fundamentally changes their attitude to a number of their fellow human beings.

The first indication in that direction is readily offered by the mass of publications and articles on "identity" in many countries. What is certain and evident, is rarely discussed. The simple fact that one starts to discuss this and related issues, indicates that they have ceased to be self-evident, that they are becoming problematic. This is generally accompanied by a process of growing awareness. Especially in countries where different peoples live together, there is talk of national, regional and sub-regional identities. But the crucial question always involves the nature of "the identity of the collective self": does language constitute identity? Does culture constitute identity? And so on.

As we have seen, history plays an important role in this respect. The more uncertain the identity of the collective self becomes, the more welcome is information and literature that can confirm that identity. Conversely, authors who demonstrate during this period that the collective identity is mostly founded on (historical) myths are extremely dysfunctional, especially for the more conservative public. Viewed from a more institutional perspective, it is clear that there are political parties that feed on the need for

6 Compare: R. Munting, *An economic and social history of gambling in Britain and the USA*. Manchester and New York, Manchester University Press, 1996.

Illustration 6.30: 1980, 38

Illustration 6.31: 1983, 50

the confirmation of collective identity. More explicitly, the European Union even has a Union of the Regions, which meets precisely this need. With the end of the USSR, the question has become paramount in that part of the world too, but it can be argued that totally different reasons are at play there — reasons which have little to do with the long waves, but rather result from the prolonged suppression of the national identities by communism.

These periods of high uncertainty about the identity of the collective self also testify to another, intensely irrational but greatly psychological reflex, namely the growing intolerance towards all those who are not inclusive to the collective identity: those who have a different political-social-religious identity, who differ by purely "race" characteristics, or who belong to groups — e.g. homosexuals — which slight certain norms of behaviour (which at that moment are very important).

The increased basic anxiety towards the lowest point of the long wave thus affects identity in two, intimately interconnected ways: as the understanding and the focus of the characteristics of the identity of the collective self diminish, groups with recognisably different identities are experienced as a threat and therefore more radically pushed away. This then is the nucleus of the mass reception of xenophobia, anti-Semitism, racism, etc. In contrast, the return of self-confidence in the ascending long wave involves a growing tolerance towards other languages, colours, races, opinions, behaviours, belief systems, etc., to the point that many accept and promote this tolerance as an essential social virtue. The extreme conservatives then speak of permissiveness.

To test this segment of the hypothesis, the immediate results can, arguably, be expected from the mapping of the research on the great waves of anti-Semitism (probably the best documented form of xenophobia) onto the proposed framework of the long waves.

17. Nature as an anxiety-free space?

Time and again, nature starts to play an important role in the descending or low-point phases of the long wave. During the last descending long wave, for example, it is very striking how the emergence of green movements and parties coincides exactly with the turn of the long wave in 1971. Apart from the traditional nature societies, no one in 1966 even considered fighting for the maintenance and protection of nature. But a mere five years later, green parties made their appearance in the whole of Europe. It was the first time that the interest in nature in a descending long wave was politically expressed. In the first two descending and lowest points of the Kondratiev wave, this interest had been articulated through the arts, namely in the Romantic Movement and in Jugendstil. In the third descending phase in the 1920s, there were first the *Wandervögel*, followed quickly and on a far greater scale by the confessional youth movements which centred around marches and activities in free unspoilt nature. In the most recent descending phase, the interest in nature is accompanied with the restoration of appreciation of the rural and rural life, whereby the traditional little farmers' village evolved from a relic of agrarian history to a jewel of rurality.[7]

It has to be noted that it may be problematic to assume the notion of "nature" to be identical in each of these phases. Whereas this problem needs

7 In Flanders, 1973 was proclaimed "Year of the Village." At the same time, Germany organized a competition "Our village should become more beautiful."

careful consideration, which exceeds the scope of this paper, there remains the question of the appeal of nature or, more accurately, of what is presented as nature. For a quarter of a century people walk around in nature without the latter having any allure, and then another quarter century follows in which that same reality acquires a very special meaning. It is difficult to find the explanation in that reality itself. In analogy with section 14, it can be argued that here too, a process of fictionalisation of reality takes place. The main attraction of nature for the uncertain person, with all the characteristics mentioned above, is undoubtedly that it offers a universe free of people, in which there is also movement and growth but in which all those feelings which make the life of the anxious and uncertain human so troublesome, are absent. Nature constitutes a watermark of society as one would wish it to be: peaceful and without threat. The always emotional and arguably romantic return to nature therefore only occurs if human society in the long run has lost a lot of its attractiveness because of its more uncertain and anxious perception. Friedrich Nietzsche's saying that we love nature because nature has no opinion of us perfectly fits this context.

Illustration 6.32: 1995, 48

Illustration 6.33: 1985, 37

Descending phases and lowest points of the long wave of basic anxiety are, moreover, in general, a fruitful climate for utopias of peaceful societies. In that sense, the return to nature also includes a utopian dimension.

With the fading of anxiety and uncertainty during the ascending long conjunctural wave, and thus the return of self-confidence (even self-satisfaction), the heightened emotionality, which enabled such a fictionalisation of reality, also disappears. More importantly, the need itself to flee from society disappears, as one starts to feel at home in that society again.

It must be clear that the romantic return to nature cannot be equated with the pragmatic concern for the destruction of the environment. By virtue of this romantic preoccupation with nature, the latter has received a lot of attention and has given rise to legislation that, even with the disappearance of the romantic concern, retains its validity. However, the degree to which the green political parties are based on the romantic feeling of nature as described above, will be mirrored by an equal degree of decline in their success during the ascending movement of the long wave — a development which will be paralleled by the nationalist parties. Among the green parties this became visible as the position of the "fundamentalists" weakened in favour of the "realists."

18. Renewed, but which religiosity?

Historians, and anyone with some experience of life, know the degree to which someone who lives through anxiety-inducing situations comes to be increasingly receptive to the supernatural. To some extent, this aspect has been explored in section 15; but a few examples will clarify the present context. The inclination towards the supernatural explains the reaction of a parish priest in the middle of the nineteenth century who, on entering a virtually empty church one Sunday, thought back to the time of cholera when his church was packed each Sunday. It is well documented that new soldiers who face the firing line for the first time, almost without exception appeal to a supreme being — a tendency that strongly declines after a number of battles. Very ill people also demonstrate the increasing inclination to plead for supernatural help.

Despite their recurrence, these cases do not in themselves demonstrate a trend. But it is obvious that with the increase of the average basic anxiety in society in a descending phase or in the lowest point of the long wave, the need for contacts with a supernatural higher power or a supreme power will increase. This then immediately raises the question as to whether it is indeed the case that in the past twenty five years this need has been expressed, for instance, in an increased degree of churchgoing, an increased number of vocations, etc. The answer to this question is immediate and negative — and documented by many publicised data that testify to increasing secularisation. However, this merely demonstrates that the possible increase in what could be called religiosity is not reflected in the quantitative material that refers to the traditional churches. In other words, the traditional churches have not succeeded in absorbing the metaphysical needs that result from the increased basic anxiety.

This is not to deny that within the traditional churches, this increased need has also lead to a broader adherence to more intense forms of belief, such as the charismatic movement or that the fall in vocations has been halted or at least slowed down. It is clear, however, that extra-church forms of faith were and still are on the increase. Good examples in point are the American televangelists who in the past quarter of a century have experienced a fantastic boom and currently reach millions of followers. Another example, for which, unfortunately, little statistical material is available, is the success of numerous sects, the existence of which not only becomes known to the larger public by the exposure of abuses. Of even greater value for this study would be longitudinal quantitative material on the many and diverse forms of popular belief which in themselves and in terms of theology are perhaps not that important, but which are extremely apt yardsticks for the study of the increase or decrease over a long term in the average basic anxiety in society.

By relating increasing uncertainty and anxiety with religiosity, the general argument presented is that it is maintained that in this correlation too, anxiety plays an important role — an idea that in itself is not new. The novelty lies merely in the hypothesis of the longitudinal occurrence of religiosity in the explanatory framework of the long waves of basic anxiety. And if the hypothesis is correct, the coming phase will be one of far-reaching secularisation which will not primarily affect the traditional churches, but most certainly the extra-church faiths.

Illustration 6.34: 1994, 52

Illustration 6.35: 19-06-1972

19. A fin de siècle every half century

There is one period in the last two centuries in which the frame of mind of the lowest point of the long wave of basic anxiety has been described, both very explicitly and on very different levels, and that is the end of the 19th century. As a reminder, the lowest point of that descending phase was, according to Kondratiev, 1896. The fact that that general state of world fatigue coincidentally occurred at the end of the century, has led to its association with that turn. The result has been that the association between world fatigue and the end of the century has become fixed in peoples' mind. As the lowest point of the current long wave again occurred just before the turn of the century, the affinity with the end of the last century was soon suggested, and one inadvertently gave the impression that the general atmosphere of world fatigue, hopelessness, even pessimism, is a perpetual problem, somehow related to the turn of centuries.

Such reasoning evidently denies the crucial question to be posed, namely that of how the fact that a year "suddenly" ends with two zeros can have such a far-reaching influence on the mental climate of a period. The explanatory framework presented here not only accommodates the question; it also proffers the explanation: the lowest point of the long wave twice coincidentally occurred before the turn of a century. This, however, immediately raises the next question, of the other two lowest points, those that did not occur at the end of a century, namely the low point of 1847 and that of the early 1930s. In terms of their general mental climate, both were extremely sombre periods which under closer scrutiny have many points in common with both turns of the century, as is demonstrated in the longitudinal studies which go sufficiently far back in time.

Illustration 6.36: 1996, 1

The explanation must be that the latter two periods were not connected with clearly recognisable time markers, which has meant that the memory of the recurrent character of the intermediate fin de siècle has been lost — something which has not been the case for the fin de siècle which actually occurred at the turn of a century.

20. Everyday life

Everyday life is ordinary life with all its routine actions, its day-to-day worries, the time we work, the time we relax, eat, laugh and joke, the times of action and of idleness, and so on, the most commonplace actions we can think of — and which we hardly ever think back to. Everyday life is quite important, as it is the greater part of our lives. The opposite of everyday life is the exceptional, the festive and the singular, which we spontaneously continue to remember.

Living the everyday life is also a specific state of mind. We experience our own commonplace everyday life in a particular way, even though we are not always conscious of it. On Freud's pleasure/displeasure scale, we could say, everyday life is simply normal, ordinary, but somehow it feels nice or, on the other hand, simply commonplace, but tense in some way, insecure. We could call it the "keynote" of our state of mind in everyday life. Surely, one way or another, everyone has experienced that the keynote of his or her state of mind changes. One loses one's job and from one day to the next, the keynote of everyday life becomes less pleasurable. To a student, the keynote sounds different before the exams and after. We are talking here about a fact that is more basic than, for example, the good mood at a party, or the bad mood that overcomes someone who gets a puncture.

Now, we can quite reasonably assume that in a descending long wave, in a period of increasing uncertainty and existential anxiety, the keynote of the state of mind of a whole population is different from that in an ascending phase of the same long wave, in which self-assurance and self-confidence and all other states of mind that are typical of this begin to get the upper hand.

The question now is not what this keynote consists of, how it is formed, how quickly or slowly it changes, etcetera, although this may have its importance. We need this notion only to make a distinction — a floating distinction of course — between everyday life during a descending phase and during an ascending phase of a single long wave of anxiety. While in the ascending phase, the keynote shows ever-stronger signs of uncertainty and existential anxiety, and everyday life — the *hic and nunc* — becomes increasingly displeasing. Some people will seek escape routes from the conscious experience of the present. They fill their consciousness with other worlds: dreams, fiction, films, drugs, alcohol, exotic travel, eccentric actions, unsafe behaviour, in one word, escapist behaviour. At these moments, escapism is extremely functional with respect to the underlying mindset as it helps suppress the displeasing keynote.

However, as soon as they fall from the heights of the long wave of anxiety — once the uncertainty begins to ebb away from the keynote of everyday life — everyday life becomes increasingly pleasant again. This means that all those escapist mechanisms stop being functional, due to the absence of a keynote that demands them. It means, for example, that it can again be pleasant to be on one's own, be bored, and laze about. The other individualism, that of the self-assured person, which again begins to take shape during the descending long wave of anxiety — that is, the more positive experience of oneself — largely contributes to it and, in fact, forms part of it. It is as if people become familiar again with their everyday life, and accept it as it is, in a positive way.

Actually, we can see this reversal of the attitude towards everyday reality on a more general level, i.e. as the reversal of the attitude towards concrete reality such as it manifests itself to the individual. This amounts in fact to a change of fundamental escapism — the negative attitude towards reality, the golden age of doom-mongers — into a positive attitude towards reality, a reality-friendly attitude, a positive realism. Today, at the beginning of the 21st century, this reversal begins slowly but surely to become manifest.

The question is how to detect this change in contemporary society and see it progress, and how this reversal has manifested itself in previous long waves.

As for contemporary society, voyeuristic reality soaps on television seem to be a symptom: we are no longer watching escapist fiction but everyday life — be it extremely artificial, yet extremely banal everyday life — and it achieves very high ratings. We must observe this phenomenon, keeping this question at the back of our minds: which changes should appear in the keynote before we consider this kind of spectacle as functional with regard to the needs of millions of people? There is only one answer: reality, everyday life, begins to gain importance again, which nourishes the interest in everyday life, i.e. in reality in general.

Bibliography

ADLER, A., *Lebenskenntnis*. Frankfurt/Main, 1978.

AFTALION, A., *The Theory of Economic Cycles Based on the Capitalistic Technique of Production*. In: The Review of Economic Statistics, 9, 1927.

AFTALION, A., *Les crises générales et périodiques de surproduction*. Paris, 1913, 2 vols.

ALEXANDER, J.C., *Neofunctionalism and After*. Malden-Oxford, 1998.

BARNETT V., *Kondratiev and the Dynamics of Economic Development. Long Cycles and Industrial Growth in Historical Context*. Houndmills, 1998.

BARRO R. J., (ed.), *Modern Business Cycle Theory*. Oxford, 1989.

BECK, A.T., *Cognitive Therapy and the Emotional Disorders*, New York, 1976.

BILZ, R., *Der Subjektzentrismus im Erleben der Angst*. In: H. VON DITFURTH, (ed.), Aspekte der Angst. Stuttgart, 1965, pp.109-117.

BOURCIER DE CARBON, L., *Démographie et conjoncture*. In: L'Année sociologique, 1978, 29, pp. 9-39.

BUTOLLO, W., *Die Angst ist eine Kraft. Über die konstruktive Bewältigung der Alltagsängsten*. München, Zürich, 2nd ed., 1984.

BUTOLLO, W., *Chronische Angst. Theorie und Praxis der Konfrontationstherapie*. München, 1979.

CHAPMAN, A.H., *Harry Stack Sullivan. His life and his work*. New York, 1976.

COENEN-HUTHER, J., *Le fonctionnalisme en sociologie: et après ?* Bruxelles, 1984.

COFER, C.N., APPLEY, M.H., *Motivation: Theory and Research*. New York, London, Sidney, 1964.

COHEN, G.A., *Karl Marx's Theory of History*. Oxford, 1978.

COLOMY, P., (ed.), *Functionalist Sociology*. Aldershot-Brookfield, 1990, 2 vols.

CONDRAU, G., *Angst und Schuld als Grundprobleme der Psychotherapie*. Bern, Stuttgart, 1962.

COURTHEOUX, J.-P., *Observations sur violence et mouvement économique*. In : L'Année sociologique, 1978, 29, pp. 159-189.

DAVIS, M., *Psychological Interpretations of Society*. New York, 1929.

DE LANDTSHEER, C., *Theoretische en empirische studie van de politieke taal. Toepassing: de politieke taal in de Vlaamse media (1831-1981)*. Gent, 1985 (Not published Ph. D.-thesis).

DENZIN, N.K., *On Understanding Emotion*. San Francisco, Washington, London, 1984.

DHONDT, J., *L'histoire récurrente*. In :Diogène. Revue internationale des sciences humaines (Paris), 1971, 75, pp. 26-59

DIAZ-ANDREU, M. & CHAMPION, T., (eds.), *Nationalism and Archeology in Europe*. London, 1996.

DUMON, W., *Causes and effects of the new patterns of fertility and family formation: sociological interpretations and expectations for the future*. In: S. FELD, R. LESTHAEGHE, 1984.

DURKHEIM, E., *Les règles de la méthode sociologique*. Paris, 1895; De sociologische methode. Ingeleid door prof. dr. E. Leemans. Antwerpen, Rotterdam, 1969.

EATWELL, J., MILGATE, M., NEWMAN, P., (eds.), *The New Palgrave. A Dictionnary of Economics*. London, Basingstoke, New York, 1987, 4 vols.

ELIAS, N., *Über den Prozess der Zivilisation*, 1939.

ELLIS Valentine, *Business Cycles and Forecasting*. 8th ed., Cincinnati, 1991.

Erich FROMM, *Escape from Freedom*. New York, 1941.

FEDDER,J.,(=J.van Gelderen), *Springvloed. Beschouwingen over industriële ontwikkeling en prijsbewegingen*. In: De Nieuwe Tijd, 18, 1913.

FELD, R., LESTHAEGHE, R., (eds.), *Demografie en toekomstverkenning*. Brussel, 1984.

FESTY, P., *Evolution contemporaine du mode de formation des familles en Europe Occidentale*. In : European Journal of Population, 1, 1985, pp. 179-205.

FISCHER David Hackett, *The Great Wave. Price Revolutions and the Rhythm of History*. New York, Oxford, 1996.

FISCHER Irving, *The Purchasing Power of Money*. 2nd ed., 1913.

FITZGERALD,R., (ed.), *Human Needs and Politics*. Rushcutters Bay, 1977.

FORDYN, A., *Het wetenschappelijk onderzoek van politieke aanslagen: een nieuwe dimensie*. In: Tijdschrift voor Sociale Wetenschappen, 1981, 1, pp. 3-20.

FORRESTER, N.B., *The Life Cycle of Economic Development*. Cambridge (Mass.), 1973.

FRASER, I., *Hegel and Marx. The Concept of Need*. Edinburgh, 1998.

FREEMAN Christopher, (ed.), *Long Wave Theory*. Cheltenham, UK, Brookfield, US, 1996.

FRIJDA Nico H., *The Emotions*. Cambridge, 1986.

FRÖHLICH, W.D., *Angst. Gefahrensignale und ihre psychologische Bedeutung*. München, 1982.

FROMM, E., *Escape from Freedom*. New York, 1941.

FUKUYAMA, Francis, *The End of History and the Last Man*. Penguin Books, 1992.

GAUS, H., WITTE, E., *L'histoire, science du comportement*. In : Revue belge d'histoire contemporaine, IV, 1973, 3-4, pp. 475-501.

GAUS, H., *The Function of Fiction. An Investigation Into the Relation Between the Reader's Real World and the Fictional World of His Reading*. Gent, 1979.

GAUS, H., *Menselijk gedrag tijdens langdurige economische recessies. Een schets*. Malle, 1982, 2. Ausg. 1984.

GAUS, H., VAN HOE, J., BRACKELEIRE, M., *Mensen en Mode. De relatie tussen kleding en konjunktuur*. Leuven, Apeldoorn, 1992, 3rd ed., 1998.

GAUS, H., *Gedragsfunctionalisme als methode van waarneming en als aanzet tot verklaring*. In: Demokritos, 1999,4.

GAUS, H., *Fluctuaties op de fictionele markt*. In: Het boek in Vlaanderen 2000-2001. Antwerpen, 2000.

GLASNER David, *Business Cycles and Depressions. An Encyclopedia*. New York, London, 1997.

GOLDSTEIN, Joshua S., *Long Cycles. Prosperity and War in the Modern Age*. New Haven, London, 1988.

GOULDNER, A.W., *Reciprocity in Functional Theory*. In: N.J. DEMERATH, R.A. PETERSON, (eds.), System, Change and Conflict. New York, 1967, pp. 141-169.

HELLER, A., *Theorie der Bedürfnisse bei Marx*. Berlin-West, 1976.

HORNEY, K., *The Neurotic Personality of Our Time*. New York, London, 1964 (1937).

IZARD, C.E., *Anxiety: A Variable Combination of Interacting Fundamental Emotions*. In: Ch. SPIELBERGER, 1972.

JASNY, N., *Soviet Economists of the Twenties: Names to be remembered*. Cambridge, 1972.

KEYNES, J.M., *The General Theory of Employment, Interest and Money*. London, 1936.

KIERKEGAARD, S., *Der Begriff der Angst*. 1844.

KIRCHGÄSSNER, W., *Probleme der Einheit von Rationalem und Emotionalem im Erkenntnisprozess*. Berlin, Akademie-Verlag, 1971.

KLEINKNECHT, A., MANDEL, E., WALLERSTEIN, I., (eds.), *New Findings in Long-Wave Research*. London, New York, 1992.

KONDRATIEFF, N. D. *Die langen Wellen der Konjunktur*. In: Archiv für Sozialwissenschaft und Sozialpolitik, 56, 1926, pp. 573-610.

KROEBER, A.L., *On the Principle of Order in Civilization as Exemplified by Change of Fashion*. In: American Anthropologist, 21, 1919, pp. 235-263.

KUCZYNSKI, Th., *Marx and Engels on Long Waves*. In: T. VASKO, (ed.), *The Long Wave Debate*. Berlin, 1987.

LAPLANCHE, J., *L'angoisse*. 2nd ed., Paris, 1981.

LASH, C., *The Culture of Narcissism. American Life in an Age of Diminishing Expectations*. New York, 1979.

LASSWELL, H.D., *Psychopathology and Politics*. Chicago, 1931.

LASSWELL, H.D., *The Triple Appeal Principle. A Contribution of Psychoanalysis to Political and Social Science*. In: American Journal of Sociology, 1931-32, vol. 37.

LEDERER, K., (ed.), *Human Needs. A Contribution to the Current Debate*. Cambridge, Mas., 1980.

LENOIR, M., *Etudes sur la formation et le mouvement des prix*. Paris,1913.

LESCURE, J., *Hausses et baisses des prix de longue durée*. Paris, 1933.

LESTER, D., *Domestic Integration and Suicide in 21 Nations, 1950-1985*. In: International Journal of Comparative Sociology, 1994, 1-2.

LEVITT,E.E., *The Psychology of Anxiety*. London, 1968.

LÜSCHER, M., *Die Lüscher-Würfel. Zur Selbsterfahrung und Persönlichkeitsbeurteilung*. 2nd ed., Düsseldof, Wien, New York, 1991.

LÜSCHER, M., *Signale der Persönlichkeit. Rollen-Spiele und ihre Motive. Völlig überarbeitete. und ergänzte Neuausgabe*. Düsseldof, Wien, New York, 1996.

MADDISON, A., *Dynamic Forces in Capitalist Development. A Long Run Comparative View*. Oxford, 1991.

MAGER, N.H., *The Kondratieff Waves*. New York, 1987.

MALINOWSKI, B., *A Scientific Theory of Culture and Other Essays*. Chapel Hill, 1944.

MANDEL, E., *Long Waves of Capitalist Development. The Marxist Interpretation*. Cambridge, 1980.

MANNHEIM Karl, *An Introduction to the Study of Society*. Edited by J.S. Erös and W.A.C. Stewart. New York, 1957.

MASLOW, A.H., *Motivation and Personality*. 2nd ed., New York, 1970.

MATTHEWS, W., *British Autobiographies. An Annotated Bibliography of British Autobiographies Published or Written Before 1951*. Berkeley, 1955.

MATTHEWS, W., *British diaries. An Annotated Bibliography of British Diaries Written Between 1442 and 1942*. Berkeley, 1950.

MAY, R., *The Meaning of Anxiety*. New York, 1950.

MERTON, R.K., *Social Theory and Social Structure. Revised and enlarged edition*. Glencoe, 1957.

MITCHELL, B.R., *International Historical Statistics. Europe, 1750-1988*. London, 1996.

MITCHELL, B.R., *International Historical Statistics. The Americas, 1750-1988*. New York, 1993.

MITSCHERLICH, Alexander & Margarete, *Die Unfähigkeit zu trauern. Grundlagen kollektiven Verhaltens*. München, 1967.

MÜLLER, J.B., *Bedürfnis*. In: O.BRUNNER, W.CONZE, R.KOSELLECK, Geschichtliche Grundbegriffe, Vol. I, Stuttgart, 1972, pp. 440-489.

MUNTING, R., *An economic and social history of gambling in Britain and the USA*. Manchester & New York, Manchester University Press, 1996.

PARETO, V., *Forme di fenomeni economici e previsioni*. In:Rivista di scienza bancaria. 1917 ; Faits et théories. Genève, 1976.

PEART, S.J., *Sunspots and Expectations. W.S.Jevon's Theory of Economic Fluctuations*. In: Journal of the History of Economic Thought, 13, 1991, pp.243-265.

PETZINA, D., VAN ROON, G., (eds.), *Konjunktur, Krise, Gesellschaft. Wirtschaftliche Wechsellagen und soziale Entwicklung im 19. und 20. Jahrhundert*. Stuttgart, 1981.

RAY, J.J., *Race and Climate as Influences on Anxiety*. (1983).

REBER, A.S., *The Penguin Dictionary of Psychology*. 1985.

REICH, W., *Die Massenpsychologie des Faschismus*. Berlin, 1971 (1933).

REIJNDERS, J., *Long Waves in Economic Development*. Aldershot, U.K., 1990, 296p.

REIJNDERS, J., *Pioneers of Long Waves Research: Van Gelderen, Kondratieff and the Intellectual Heritage of Tugan-Baranowski*. In: Economies et Sociétés, 27, 1993, 7-8, pp.261-93.

RICHARDSON, J., KROEBER, A.L., *Three Centuries of Women's Dress Fashion. A Quantitative Analysis*. In: Anthropological Records, 5, 1940, pp. 111-153.

RICHTER, H.-E., *Umgang mit Angst*. Hamburg, 1992.

RIESMAN, D., GLAZER, N., DENNY, R., *The Lonely Crowd*. Garden City, 1955.

RUBINS, J.L., *Karen Horney. Gentle Rebel of Psychoanalysis*. London, 1978.

SAPIR, E., *The Uncounscious Patterning of Behavior in Society*. In: CHILD, C.M., KOFFKA, K., et al., The Uncounscious. A Symposium. New York, 1928.

SCANDELLA Luigi, *Le Kondratieff. Essai de théorie des cycles longs économiques et politiques*. Paris, 1998.

SCHULZE, G., *Die Erlebnisgesellschaft. Kultursoziologie der Gegenwart*. Frankfurt-New York, 1992.

SCHUMPETER, J.A., *Business Cycles. A Theoretical, Historical and Statistical Analysis of the Capitalist Process*. 2 vols., New York-London, 1939.

SEVENS, J., *Evolutie van de belangstelling voor de dood in Engeland, Frankrijk, Duitsland en de V.S.A. 1850-1980.* In: Tijdschrift voor Sociale Wetenschappen, 1987, 1, pp. 24-50.

SHERMAN Howard J., *The Business Cycle. Growth and Crisis under Capitalism.* Princeton, 1991.

SOPER, K., *On Human Needs. Open and Closed Theories in an Marxist Perspective.* Brighton, 1981.

SÖRENSEN, M., *Einführung in die Angstpsychologie.* 4th ed., Weinheim, 1996.

SOROKIN, P.A., *Man and Society in Calamity. The Effects of War, Revolution, Famine, Pestilence upon Human Mind, Behavior, Social Organization and Cultural Life.* New York, 1942.

SPENGLER, Oswald, *Der Untergang des Abendlandes. Umrisse einer Morphologie der Weltgeschichte.* 2 vols. (1918-1922), München, 1990.

SPIELBERGER, Ch., (ed.), *Anxiety. Current Trends in Theory and Research.* Vol. I., New York, London, 1972.

STERNLIEB, G., HUGHES, J.W., *The Demographic Long Wave: Population Trends and Economic Growth.* In: Economic Development Quarterly, 1987, 4, pp. 307-322.

STOCKING, G.W. Jr., (ed.), *Functionalism Historicised. Essays on British Social Anthropology.* Madison, Wisconsin, 1984.

STURMEY, P., *Functional Analysis in Clinical Psychology.* Chichester, 1996.

VAN DUIJN, J.J., *De lange golf in de economie. Kan innovatie ons uit het dal helpen.* Assen, 1979; The Long Waves in Economic Life. London, 1983.

VAN RAALTEN, F., *Angst. Een wijsgerig-antropologische beschouwing.* Bussum, 1981.

VASKO, T., (ed.), *The Long Wave Debate.* Berlin, 1987.

VESTDIJK, S., *Het wezen van de angst.* Den Haag, Amsterdam, 1968.

VON BAEYER-KATTE, W., *Furcht und Angst.* In: Sowjetsystem und demokratische Gesellschaft. Eine vergleichende Enzyklopedie. Freiburg, Basel, Wien, Vol.II, 1968.

WALLAS, G., *The Great Society. A Psychological Analysis.* London-New York, 1920.

Index of names